MAROON COMMUNITIES IN SOUTH CAROLINA

MAROON COMMUNITIES IN SOUTH CAROLINA

A DOCUMENTARY RECORD

EDITED BY TIMOTHY JAMES LOCKLEY

THE UNIVERSITY OF SOUTH CAROLINA PRESS

© 2009 University of South Carolina

Published by the University of South Carolina Press
Columbia, South Carolina 29208

www.sc.edu/uscpress

Manufactured in the United States of America

18 17 16 15 14 13 12 11   10 9 8 7 6 5 4 3 2

Library of Congress Cataloging-in-Publication Data

Maroon communities in South Carolina : a documentary record / edited by Timothy James Lockley.
    p. cm.
   Includes bibliographical references and index.
   ISBN 978-1-57003-776-4 (cloth : alk. paper) — ISBN 978-1-57003-777-1 (pbk. : alk. paper)
   1. Maroons—South Carolina—History—Sources. 2. Fugitive slaves—South Carolina—History—Sources. 3. Community life—South Carolina—History—18th century—Sources. 4. Community life—South Carolina—History—19th century—Sources. 5. South Carolina—History—1775–1865—Sources. 6. South Carolina—Race relations—History—18th century—Sources. 7. South Carolina—Race relations—History—19th century—Sources. I. Lockley, Timothy James, 1971–
   E450.M38 2008
   305.800973—dc22

                                2008030189

CONTENTS

LIST OF ILLUSTRATIONS   vi
PREFACE   vii
INTRODUCTION   ix

CHAPTER ONE   The Origins of Marronage in South Carolina   1

CHAPTER TWO   A Late Colonial Burst of Marronage, 1765–1774   16

CHAPTER THREE   Maroons in the Revolutionary and Post-Revolutionary Eras, 1775–1787   39

CHAPTER FOUR   A (Relatively) Peaceful Interlude, 1787–1812   72

CHAPTER FIVE   The Final Flourishing of Marronage, 1813–1829   78

Afterword   128

FURTHER READING   137
INDEX   139
ABOUT THE EDITOR   143

ILLUSTRATIONS

FIGURE

River swamp on South Carolina side of the Savannah River   129

MAPS

Map of North and South Carolina from surveys by Henry Mouzon and others, 1775   2

Colleton District, South Carolina, surveyed by Saml. A. Ruddock, 1820   22

Beaufort District, South Carolina, surveyed by C. Vignoles and H. Ravenel, 1820   34

Detail from map of South Carolina and part of Georgia, from surveys by William Bull and others, 1780   37

Sketch of Georgia's northern frontiers by Archibald Campbell, 1780   43

Detail from map of South Carolina and part of Georgia   89

Georgetown District, South Carolina, surveyed by Wm. Hemingway, 1820   94

Charleston District, South Carolina, surveyed by Charles Vignoles and Henry Ravenel, 1820   109

PREFACE

This book is about maroon communities formed by runaway slaves in South Carolina. It is intended to be used by students, teachers, and academics to give them an understanding of the nature of these communities and how they differed from similar communities formed elsewhere in the Americas. The introduction provides a brief overview of the maroon societies created by runaway slaves in the Caribbean, Central and South America, and parts of North America other than South Carolina. This overview places South Carolina in the context of other New World slave societies and encourages the reader to consider how and why South Carolina was distinctive. The book is arranged chronologically. The first chapter charts the origins of marronage (the act of running away to form a maroon community) in South Carolina up to c. 1750. Chapter 2 concentrates on major episodes of marronage from the 1760s to 1774. The focus in chapter 3 is on maroons during the American Revolution and its aftermath, when marronage posed a significant threat to the peace and security of both South Carolina and Georgia. Between the late 1780s and 1812 there was a lull in maroon activity, which is the subject of chapter 4. Chapter 5 examines the late flowering of maroon activity from 1813 through the 1820s.

In order to maximize the usefulness of this collection of documentary sources, I have included relevant information to contextualize the documents for those who might not have detailed knowledge of the wider history of colonial and antebellum South Carolina. In the brief afterword I offer some of my own thoughts on marronage in South Carolina. I have not modernized or standardized the spelling or punctuation of the original documents, since part of the fun of working with primary sources is deciphering their meanings.

This book would not have been written without the encouragement and support offered by numerous friends and colleagues. Particular thanks must go to Gad Heuman, Mark Smith, Alex Moore, Hunt Boulware, and Ryan Quintana; my students Lydia Plath and Alex Chapman; staff members of the South Carolina Historical Society, the Charleston Library Society, the South Caroliniana

Library, and the South Carolina Department of Archives and History, who were enormously helpful and patient with my copying requests; and the British Academy, which had sufficient faith to generously fund my research visits to the United States. Naturally, the love and support of Jo, Alice, and Edward make the whole thing worthwhile. This book is for them.

INTRODUCTION

Maroon Communities in the New World

The word "maroon" is an English corruption of the Spanish word *cimarron,* meaning "wild, not tame," and was originally applied to livestock that had escaped from farms to run free in the woods.[1] Since first Native American and later imported African slaves were other forms of personal property that fled from plantations in Spanish colonies to remote mountainous areas, they too earned the label *cimarron.* When Sir Francis Drake traveled through Panama in 1572, he encountered people he termed "Symerons (a blacke people, which about eightie yeeres past, fled from the *Spaniards* their Masters, by reason of their crueltie, and since grown into an nation, under two Kings of their owne)."[2] These Panamanian maroons were instrumental in helping Drake and other English sailors plunder Spanish treasure convoys and generally harass the Spanish authorities.

It is important to distinguish between the vast majority of slave runaways and maroons. Although runaways formed maroon communities, many more slaves fled from bondage than ever became maroons, and the transition from runaway to maroon involved several stages. Many runaway slaves left their plantations only for short periods of time and were either caught or returned voluntarily after a few days or weeks. Not all slaves possessed the skills to fend for themselves in the woods or swamps, and once hunger became paramount in the mind of a runaway, returning to the plantation to face punishment was, for some, preferable to starvation. Slaveholders sometimes advertised their willingness to "forgive" runaway slaves who returned to their labors of their own accord, and temporary absence lasting a few days became a common way for enslaved laborers to express their discontent. Maroons, on the other hand, had no intention of returning to slavery. They set out to form independent communities that were self-sufficient and that could exist outside of the systems of government created by Europeans in the Americas.

Maroon communities arose wherever slavery took hold in the Americas. As early as the 1540s sizable groups of several hundred runaway slaves had formed their own communities away from European colonists in Cuba and Santo Domingo. By the seventeenth century, as slavery increased its stranglehold among the societies of the New World, maroon communities emerged on the mainland of South and Central America in Brazil and Colombia and on some of the smaller Caribbean islands such as Antigua. The eighteenth century saw marronage reach its greatest extent in Jamaica, Surinam, and Brazil with large and well-organized groups of maroons able to defend their independence by military means against the attempts of European colonizers to defeat them.

Maroon Communities in Spanish America

The Spanish were the first Europeans to establish themselves in the New World, seizing control first of the major Caribbean islands of Hispaniola, Cuba, and Jamaica before conquering Mexico and Peru, the two most sophisticated Native American civilizations in the Americas.[3] In order to exploit the natural resources on the mainland the Spanish turned to forced labor, initially using conquered native peoples but later importing African slaves. It was not long before runaway slaves, often with the support and guidance of disaffected Native Americans, started to band together to form maroon communities, termed *palenques* by the Spanish, in mountainous, densely forested, or swampy areas where there were few Spanish settlers. These *palenques* were a thorn in the side of Spanish authorities because not only did they act as a magnet for other slaves who might flee from their masters, but they also had an impact on outlying settlements. Unable to be totally self-sufficient, maroons traded with neighboring whites and slaves for a variety of commodities, especially guns, powder, and metal tools. Where trading was not possible, or was prevented by slaveholders, the maroons raided plantations and simply took what they wanted. For this reason Spanish authorities frequently mounted military expeditions against the *palenques*, but these were only partly successful. The Spanish first had to find the maroon communities, and since *palenques* were usually secreted away in remote and inaccessible areas, this was not easy. The Native Americans present among the maroons provided vital local knowledge as to the best locations for settlements that were both defensible and had ready supplies of fresh water. Maroons also consciously made their settlements hard to find by laying false trails, with traps for the unwary, and jealously guarding the locations of their towns by, for instance, not permitting new arrivals to leave until they had proved themselves trustworthy and never bringing strangers to their towns.

If the Spanish were able to pinpoint the precise location of a maroon settlement, perhaps from a captured member of the community, they then had to mount a successful attack against well-fortified defensive positions. Maroons were often able to fight off attacks from regular troops, and when the Spanish were on occasion able to storm a town and destroy it, significant numbers of maroons simply melted away into the wilderness to re-form their community elsewhere. As Spanish troops traveled back to their towns they were often harried by maroons skilled in guerrilla warfare. Ambushes and traps claimed the lives of many Spanish soldiers.

Given the difficulty of permanently eradicating maroon communities once they had become established, Spanish authorities tried a different approach. In 1609, having tried and failed to destroy one particularly large *palenque* near Vera Cruz that had existed since the 1570s, Mexican authorities came to an agreement with a maroon leader named Yanga. They would acknowledge the free status of the maroons under his command and permit them to live undisturbed in their own town, and in return, Yanga promised that his people would help to capture and return other runaways that might flee to them. This evolution of Spanish policy toward maroon communities was copied in other parts of Spanish America. In Cuba, Colombia, and elsewhere in Mexico, for instance, early maroon communities were invariably attacked in an attempt to destroy them before they could become well established. If those assaults failed (while some were successful, many were not), then gradually local authorities came to some sort of formal accommodation with the maroons, recognizing their de facto freedom in return for military help against enemies or for promises of help in the capture of other runaway slaves. Where both sides observed the agreement, then it was possible for the maroon community either to become gradually assimilated into the wider population through trade and other forms of social interaction or to maintain its isolation and distance and thereby minimize any impact its existence might have on white society. It was therefore possible for maroon communities to persist for lengthy periods of time in the Spanish colonies.

Treaties, however, could be broken by either side, leading to renewed hostilities. Some maroons were lax in their pursuit of runaways and even accepted fugitives into their communities to boost their own numbers, while other maroons continued to raid plantations for supplies. Furthermore, some maroon communities found that their initial isolation from European settlements disappeared as Spanish settlements expanded. The encroachment of new Spanish settlers onto what maroons thought was their land often triggered reprisals and subsequent military campaigns by the Spanish in order to protect their countrymen. Maroon communities that had endured for many decades were sometimes destroyed when they came in conflict with expanding Spanish settlements, and only a small number of maroon settlements in the remotest areas lasted until the end of slavery.

Maroon Communities in Surinam

Of the three European powers that established colonies in the Guianas (Britain, Holland, and France), it was the Dutch colony of Surinam that prospered most during the eighteenth century.[4] The massive importation of slaves to grow sugar, coffee, and later cotton encouraged the emergence of a fully developed, and highly repressive, slave society. The concentration of plantations near the coast meant that runaway slaves found a ready, safe haven in the dense jungles of the interior. From the mid-seventeenth century to the mid-eighteenth century thousands of enslaved people fled one of the most brutal slave regimes in the Americas. The settlements formed by these maroons were usually grouped around one of the numerous rivers that ran from the south of the country to the northern coast and gradually became grouped into a smaller number of "tribes" of what the Dutch authorities termed "bush negroes."

Concerned about the example these "tribes" set for slaves remaining on the plantations and the tempting alternative to slavery they effectively offered, Dutch authorities tried their best to destroy them. Numerous expeditions of local militia units and regular troops from Holland were dispatched against the various "tribes," but they invariably suffered enormous casualties, as much from disease and malnutrition as from battles with the maroons. Major maroon settlements were not only inaccessible; they were also well defended with traps. Accepting that they would never completely destroy the maroons—one governor likened them to a Hydra: no matter how many were killed, more fresh runaways always replaced them—authorities decided to make peace. Treaties were made with the major tribes from the 1760s onward, confirming their freedom in return for promises to aid in the capture of new runaways. Several planters believed that these treaties were a sign of weakness; yet the Dutch aim was to prevent further challenges to the slave system, and in this they largely succeeded. The tribes of "bush negroes" effectively lived in a world that was isolated from that of whites and retained a strong African culture that persists to this day. Unlike some other maroon bands in the Americas, the "bush negroes" of Surinam had the good fortune to remain away from plantation areas and so avoid the assimilation that was common for maroons in Spanish territories.

Maroon Communities in French Colonies

Marronage existed in all of the French possessions in the New World, but in most of them, such as Guadeloupe, Martinique, Grenada, and St. Kitts, the small size of the islands and the nature of the terrain meant that maroons never posed a serious threat to peace and stability.[5] Maroon groups were usually small and existed by predatory raiding of neighboring plantations, but where groups were well entrenched in mountainous areas, such as in Martinique in 1665, local authorities followed the Spanish model of signing peace treaties with the maroons.

The largest and most enduring maroon communities in French territory occurred not in the largest territory—French Guiana—but in St. Domingue (Haiti). The limited economic development of French Guiana, compared with neighboring Surinam, and the relatively small number of slaves ensured that marronage was never a major issue in Cayenne and its hinterlands, though in the late eighteenth century French authorities did have to deal with maroons who fled to French Guiana from Surinam. In Haiti, however, the French created a slave society to rival those in Cuba, Jamaica, Bahia, and South Carolina. Hundreds of thousands of slaves toiled to grow sugar and other staples, and inevitably some of them fled their bondage to form maroon communities in the mountainous interior. One of the longest-lasting groups was Le Maniel, on the border of French St. Domingue and Spanish San Domingo. The Spanish tolerated the presence of this group on the border of their territory and even traded with them because their mere existence was a check on any possible designs the French might have had to the entire island of Hispaniola. When the French periodically launched military strikes against Le Maniel, the maroons simply slipped across the border into Spanish territory during the raid, returning once the French troops had left. For most of the eighteenth century the maroons of Le Maniel were left alone, but increasing encroachment by French coffee plantations on what the maroons had come to see as their land elevated tensions in the 1770s and 1780s.

The Haitian revolution from the early 1790s onward prevented further inroads by whites into maroon territory. Historians have debated the role that maroons played in the Haitian uprising, and while runaway slaves were crucial to the eventual success of this revolution, it is doubtful that older maroon groups such as those at Le Maniel played a decisive role. The rebellion started on the sugar plantations of the north coast of Haiti, not in the coffee plantation areas adjacent to maroon settlements. Perhaps the greatest influence that maroons had on the Haitian revolution was the example of resistance and self-determination that they set for the enslaved population. When combined with the high proportion of Africans in the slave population, and the rhetoric of liberty and equality that was rampant during the French Revolution, a uniquely unstable mix in Haiti made it ripe for revolution in 1791.

Maroon Societies in Brazil

Portuguese control of Brazil was generally limited to the coastal regions, and therefore slaves who escaped from the sugar plantations of Bahia had a vast hinterland in which to form maroon communities.[6] Numerous small maroon groups, or *quilombos*, of up to fifty people in swamps and densely forested areas close to the sugar plantation regions existed by raiding the plantations for food, equipment, and recruits. These *quilombos* differed little from the *palenques* of Cuba and Mexico and were usually little more than a small annoyance to the Portuguese authorities. Over time these *quilombos* merged into the local indigenous population and posed little threat to the society forged by Brazilian slaveholders.

Yet, Brazil was also the location for the largest and most enduring maroon community ever created in the Americas, the kingdom of Palmares. Taking advantage of the competing imperial ambitions of the Dutch and the Portuguese in northeastern Brazil, escaped slaves numbering as many as twenty thousand settled in a fairly remote mountainous region in the early seventeenth century. The numerous villages and towns that made up the community were loosely federated under a king, to whom all paid taxes to fund a centralized military force to protect the kingdom. Palmares has been described as an African kingdom in Brazil. The main settlement had several hundred dwellings and a church and was extremely well defended. Unlike their attitude toward the smaller *quilombos,* Portuguese authorities could not afford to ignore Palmares, and numerous unsuccessful military expeditions were launched from the coast to destroy it. Invariably the Portuguese fared badly fighting against maroons highly skilled in guerrilla warfare, and it was not until the Portuguese recruited mixed-race frontiersmen from southern Brazil to combat the maroons that serious inroads were made into Palmares territory. Eventually the main settlement of Palmares was captured and destroyed in 1695 and the king executed. The destruction of Palmares did not end marronage in Brazil; another extremely large *quilombo* formed in the mining region of Minas Gerais in the 1740s, and a nineteenth-century *quilombo* in Amazonia survived by trading with Dutch settlers in Surinam. Marronage was evidently something that Portuguese authorities had to deal with until the abolition of slavery in 1888.

Portuguese attitudes toward maroon communities differed from those in many other New World colonies in two respects. First, unlike the governments of Spanish, French, Dutch, and British colonies, Portuguese leaders in Brazil rarely made treaties with maroon groups. Attempts to come to some sort of accommodation with Palmares in the 1680s had failed to achieve an enduring peace, and ultimately Portuguese policy evolved into one of ignoring *quilombos* that were remote and not affecting plantations and destroying those that made a nuisance of themselves. Treaties, in the eyes of the Portuguese authorities, only gave encouragement to other slaves to flee bondage in the hope that they too would have their freedom acknowledged. Second, again unlike in other European colonies in the New World, Portuguese authorities only occasionally made use of the local Native American population as slave catchers. This was partly because they knew that natives were often sympathetic to the maroons and provided them with advance warning of impending attacks but also a recognition that most of the present-day nation of Brazil was not under Portuguese control but remained in the hands of native peoples. Indeed it was not uncommon for *quilombos* to be populated by a mixture of African and Native American peoples since both were enslaved in Brazil by the Portuguese.

Maroon Communities in the British Caribbean

The British Empire expanded in the Americas throughout the eighteenth century.[7] In the Caribbean several former French colonies, such as Grenada and St. Lucia, were added to older and more established ones, such as Barbados and Antigua. In Central and South America, British control of Belize and Guyana was gradually solidified, and on the North American mainland the defeat of the French in 1763 left Britain master of the eastern half of the continent. Slavery followed the British everywhere, but so did marronage. In Guyana, as in French Guiana, the main maroon problems came from Surinamese "bush negroes" spilling over the border, and they posed little threat to the established plantation society close to Georgetown. In many of the smaller Caribbean islands marronage was a short-lived problem due to the rapid expansion of plantation agriculture and the disappearance of forests and other remote areas where maroons could hide. On mountainous islands, such as Grenada, small maroon bands persisted but were never large enough to cause serious damage.

In Jamaica, however, conditions conspired to make the maroons a powerful and dangerous threat to English control. Slaves took advantage of the initial English invasion of the island in 1655 to flee from their Spanish masters, and for much of the next century maroons were a thorn in the side of planters and colonial officials. The number of maroons in Jamaica grew rapidly in the early eighteenth century, drawn from the thousands of African slaves who were imported by the English for their own plantations. These maroons made themselves secure in the mountainous central parts of the islands, from whence they launched raids on remote plantations for supplies of food, metal tools, and women. Attempts by militia units and regular troops to root out the maroons succeeded only in driving them to even more inaccessible parts of the island, and attempts in the 1720s to use Mosquito Indians from Central America as slave catchers also failed.

Jamaican maroons were organized into two main groups, Windward and Leeward, with little coordination between the two. Each had its own leaders and pursued its own relationship with white society. As raiding by maroons intensified in the 1720s and 1730s, what later became known as the First Maroon War broke out. Ever more strenuous efforts were made to eradicate the maroons as villages and, more importantly, crops were destroyed by troops. Yet military campaigns also cost a great deal of money, and British troops were unable to find and locate the largest and most secretive villages in the "cockpit" country of western Jamaica. Finally, in 1739, British authorities made peace overtures to the leader of the western maroons, Captain Cudjoe, which he readily accepted. In return for peace, the maroons had their freedom acknowledged and land granted for their permanent use. They were also given regular access to markets. In return, Cudjoe promised to return any new runaways who fled to his settlements. A similar agreement followed with the eastern band of maroons shortly afterward.

By all accounts these treaties were crucial for the future economic growth of the island. Whites praised the zeal of their newfound allies in returning runaways, and the slave system matured and grew into a vastly profitable one for white planters, while the maroons were left in peace to develop and grow as separate communities. Only once did this relationship break down when violence flared between one group of maroons and white authorities in the 1790s. This was by no means a general uprising by all the Jamaican maroons, but fearful of the Haitian precedent, the government of Jamaica deported these maroons to Nova Scotia in 1796 and subsequently, in 1800, to Sierra Leone.

Maroon Communities in North America

Slavery in North America never quite reached the industrial scale of that on some of the Caribbean islands. There were far more slaves in Haiti and Jamaica, for instance, than in any of the North American territories, and the relatively low level of slave imports, compared to those of other slave societies, meant that North American slaves were much more likely to be American- rather than African-born. While these factors set North America apart from other slave societies in the New World, slaves still experienced harsh repressive regimes on the tobacco plantations of Virginia, in the rice swamps of South Carolina, and in the bayous of Louisiana. Whippings, rape, and maiming were common, and so North American slaves fled their bondage, just as slaves did everywhere else in the New World. Many of these runaways were absent for just a few days before returning home, but some never came back and found safe havens in remote frontier areas away from white settlements. In 1729 the governor of Virginia reported that a group of runaway slaves had settled "in the fastness of the neighbouring mountains," and he feared that they would "very soon be encreas'd be the accession of other runaways and prove dangerous neighbours to our frontier inhabitants."[8] The intended permanency of this settlement can be seen by reports that "they had already begun to clear the ground" and that they "exchanged a shot or two" with those sent to recapture them.[9] A "very troublesome" maroon band in the heart of the tidewater in Surry County in 1787 regularly raided "smoak-houses, granaries, stables &c," and their encampment was later found to contain "horses, cooking utensils, bacon, and other provision, and in possession of the negroes, cash to the amount of 20 or 30£."[10]

The Great Dismal Swamp on the border between Virginia and North Carolina acted as a particularly strong magnet for runaway slaves. This large and otherwise deserted swamp was relatively close to the plantation regions of Virginia, and therefore it was comparatively easy for slaves to disappear into its dense forests. William Byrd came across "a family of mullatoes" in the swamp when surveying the border between the two colonies in 1728, commenting, "It is certain many slaves shelter themselves in this obscure part of the world, nor will any of their righteous neighbours discover them."[11] The German Johann Schoepf, traveling through North Carolina in 1783, reported that in the Great Dismal Swamp "small spots are to be found here and there which are always dry, and these have often been used as places of safety by runaway slaves . . . these Negro fugitives lived in security and plenty, building themselves cabins, planting corn, raising hogs and fowls which they stole from their neighbours, and naturally the hunting was free where they were."[12] John Smyth, visiting the same region the following year, agreed that "Run-away Negroes have resided in these places for twelve, twenty, or thirty years and upwards, subsisting themselves in the swamp upon corn, hogs, and fowls, that they raised on some of the spots not perpetually under water, nor subject to be flooded, as forty-nine parts of fifty of it are; and on such spots they have erected habitations, and cleared small fields around them; yet these have always been perfectly impenetrable to any of the inhabitants of the country around, even to those nearest to and best acquainted with the swamps." Consequently, runaways "in these horrible swamps are perfectly safe, and with the greatest facility elude the most diligent of their pursuers."[13]

The number of maroons in the Great Dismal Swamp can only be guessed at, though some historians have suggested that the swamp may have been home to several hundred and maybe even more than a thousand escaped slaves. Certainly maroons resided in the swamp throughout the antebellum era. One former resident of the swamp recalled that "Dar is families growed up in dat ar Dismal Swamp dat never seed a white man, an' would be skeered most to def to see one. Some runaways went dere wid dar wives, an' dar childers are raised dar." Porte Crayon encountered one such maroon in 1856 and observed that "every movement betrayed a life of habitual caution and watchfulness." The relatively small size of the swamp, about two hundred to three hundred square miles, did not afford the same opportunities for maroon community formation as did the Amazonian forests of South America or the mountains of Jamaica. Whites may not have populated the swamp itself, but they surrounded it, and there was little chance for maroons within the swamp to expand the territory under their control.[14]

Elsewhere in North Carolina smaller maroon bands took up residence in various swamps, at different times plundering plantations and causing widespread panic. In 1767 the Wilmington militia was dispatched to deal with "upwards of Twenty runaway slaves in a body arm'd," and in 1788 a captured runaway slave was summarily executed "from a supposed necessity of striking terror into a gang of runaways who infested the said Town & neighbourhood," much to the disgust of his owner. It seems that such terror tactics were not very effective, since another band near Wilmington in 1795 "in the daytime secrete[d] themselves in the swamps and woods [but] at night committed various depredations on the neighbouring plantations." This maroon group was led by a "chieftain who styled himself *The General of the Swamps*," but after he and others were killed by the militia, local white authorities were hopeful that they had broken up "this nest of miscreants."[15] Another group or groups "embodied and armed" in the southeastern corner of the state in the early 1820s spread "great alarm among the citizens" by "committing many thefts and other outrages." Of particular concern was their "increasing numbers and threatening attitude." The militias of three counties, totaling more than three hundred men, were called out against the maroons and spent more than a month in the field trying to track down and eliminate them. These efforts were only partially successful—the commander of the militia admitted that they "did not succeed in apprehending all the runaway fugitives"—but he claimed a victory of sorts "by arresting some and driving others off, and suppressing the spirit of insurrection."[16]

Local authorities in North Carolina continued to have mixed success against maroon groups for the remainder of the antebellum era. The usual pattern was that a maroon band would take up residence in a swamp and "bid defiance to any force whatever" that tried to dislodge it. Some of these encampments were sizable, with several houses, while others were far more temporary. One maroon group near Wilmington was sufficiently large to be split into three camps "plentifully supplied with provisions particularly with beef and rice" and was discovered only after "people of their own color informed against them." Another maroon group in the same region successfully deterred planters from joining patrols by singling them out for revenge attacks. A petition to the North Carolina General Assembly urging a reform of the patrol law lamented that "patrols are of no use on Account of the danger they Subject themselves to and their property. Not long since three patrols two of which for Executing their duty had their dwelling and Out houses burnt down, the Other his fodder stacks all burnt." As late as 1856 a resident of Robeson County, bordering South Carolina, complained of one "impenetrable" swamp as "a very secure retreat for runaway negroes" where "for many years past, and at this time, there are several runaways of bad and daring character destructive to all kinds of stock and dangerous to all persons living by or near said swamp." This maroon band was settled on an "island" in the swamp and "had cleared a place for a garden, had cows &c in the swamp." They were able to repulse an attack by fifteen militiamen, killing one without incurring losses themselves; then, "cursing and swearing and telling them to come on, they were ready for them again."[17]

Like their counterparts in North Carolina, slaves in French, later Spanish, Louisiana fled into the swamps and bayous bordering the plantations on the Mississippi River. For the most part the fugitives were nothing more than a minor annoyance, but in the late 1770s and early 1780s one particular group, the San Malo band, posed a particular threat to the peace and security of planters. Unlike many other maroon groups in the Americas, this one did not try to safeguard their independence by fortifying a remote hideout far from white settlements. Instead, this itinerant group frequently attacked plantations, stealing what they wanted and killing indiscriminately. They also managed to strike up a symbiotic relationship with plantation slaves, who fed and sheltered the maroons in return for help with some of their usual tasks. Facing widespread panic among their colonists, Spanish authorities eventually launched a major military expedition against the San Malo band and succeeded in capturing and executing the leading maroons.[18] In the antebellum period runaways continued to form maroon groups in the environs of New Orleans. One group of fifty or sixty maroons raised "hogs, poultry, sweet potatoes &c" in an area known as "the Trembling Praries, not far from the city . . . this spot has been supposed to be unapproachable on account of quick sands."[19] Further east along the gulf coast a maroon group secreted themselves in a swamp at the confluence of the Alabama and Tombeckbe rivers just north of Mobile. Some of the members of this group had "been runaway for several years" and were led by "an extraordinary negro for size and bodily strength" named Old Hal. Following a battle with local planters in 1827, which led to the death of several maroons, even the newspapers were forced to concede "that old Hal and his men fought like Spartans, not one gave an inch of ground, but stood and was shot dead or wounded, and fell on the spot."[20]

In another Spanish-held territory in North America, marronage was completely different. With the Spanish population of Florida never amounting to more than a few thousand, and with few slaves of their own, the Spanish authorities in Florida could afford to offer freedom and protection to runaway slaves from South Carolina and later Georgia. Indeed the Spanish hoped to destabilize British territories by actively encouraging slaves to desert. In the late 1730s Spanish authorities permitted runaway slaves to form their own settlement north of St. Augustine called Gracia Real de Santa Teresa de Mose. These maroons fought alongside the Spanish when the British invaded Florida in 1740 and were instrumental in the successful defense of St. Augustine.[21] When Spain ceded Florida to Britain in 1763, most of the maroons left for Cuba rather than risk reenslavement.

After the American Revolution, Spain recovered Florida but exercised only nominal control over much of the territory. Despite the 1790 ending of the official policy of offering sanctuary, slaves from Georgia continued to find a safe haven south of the St. Mary's River and gradually formed new maroon communities with minimal interference from the Spanish. During the War of 1812 British agents on the Apalachicola River actively recruited runaway slaves, intending to use them to harass Georgia and South Carolina. The withdrawal of the British after 1815 did not mean the end of the threat that the maroons posed, since they were left in possession of a strategically placed fort with large amounts of ammunition. An 1816 expedition by the United States Army succeeded in destroying the fort and most of its several hundred defenders, but even this did not mark the end of marronage in Florida.[22] New maroons who replaced those killed in 1816 formed an increasingly effective alliance with the Seminole Indians. During the two wars that the Seminoles fought against the United States, their maroon allies were regarded by the Americans as the more dangerous and effective enemy, inflicting several defeats on American troops.

The relationship between the Seminoles and the maroons, often termed "black Seminoles," was complex. Most maroons lived in their own villages under their own governments and paid a form of tribute to Seminole chiefs in return for nominal protection. The creole heritage of most maroons, which meant that most spoke at least some English and perhaps shared a common belief system based loosely on Christianity, set them apart from the Seminoles, who generally remained unacculturated. Maroons sometimes acted as translators and intermediaries between Seminole chiefs and white authorities, but they also took the lead in organizing military matters, knowing that military defeat would result in reenslavement. In the late 1830s the black Seminoles were removed by the army to Indian territory in present-day Oklahoma, but conflicts with other Native American groups led to a further migration to northern Mexico in the 1840s. After the Civil War, and with the threat of sale and reenslavement no longer hanging over them, many black Seminoles returned across the border to Texas. Organized as the Seminole Indian Scouts, they assisted the army against other Native American tribes. This group of maroons, who had started as runaways from plantations in Georgia and South Carolina and whose freedom had been threatened by the U.S. Army, planters, slave hunters, and other Native Americans, successfully defended themselves against them all. They can perhaps be regarded as the most successful maroon community in North America.[23]

Conclusion

For escaped slaves to form a successful maroon community in the Americas, it seems that they needed to fulfill certain criteria. First, slaves needed to live in relatively close proximity to areas such as swamps, forests, jungles, or mountains that were simultaneously inaccessible to regular troops. Second, the maroon settlement needed to be readily defensible by a small number of armed men, with limited entrances and disguised pathways to prevent accidental discovery. Third, the maroons needed to be sufficiently numerous to sustain themselves either through natural reproduction or through raiding. Fourth, they needed to have somewhere to grow food, since even in the jungle there was not enough to live on by hunting alone. Fifth, they needed to have at least some access to plantation society for trading purposes, particularly for weapons. Sixth, they needed to come to some sort of accommodation with white society, either through a peace treaty or by separating themselves so completely that they posed no serious threat to colonial regimes.

Notes

1. This definition comes from Giral del Pino, Hipólito San Joseph, *A Dictionary, Spanish and English, and English and Spanish* (London: A. Millar, J. Nourse, and P. Vaillant, 1763).

2. Philip Nicols, *Sir Francis Drake Revived* (London: William Stansby, 1628), 7.

3. See Jose L. Franco, "Maroons and Slave Rebellions in the Spanish Territories"; Francisco Perez de la Riva, "Cuban Palenques"; Aquiles Escalente, "Palenques in Colombia"; and David M. Davidson, "Negro Slave Control and Resistance in Colonial Mexico"; all are in *Maroon Societies: Rebel Slave Communities in the Americas*, 2nd ed., ed. Richard Price (Baltimore and London: Johns Hopkins University Press, 1979); Anthony McFarlane, "*Cimarrones* and *Palenques*: Runaways and Resistance in Colonial Columbia," in *Out of the House of Bondage: Runways, Resistance and Marronage in Africa and the New World*, ed. Gad Heuman (London: Frank Cass, 1986), 131–51; Patrick J. Carroll, "Mandinga: The Evolution of a Mexican Runaway Slave Community, 1735–1827," *Comparative Studies in Society and History* 19 (October 1977): 488–505; Gerald Cardoso, *Negro Slavery in the Sugar Plantations of Veracruz and Pernambuco* (Washington, D.C.: University Press of America, 1983); and Paul Lokken, "A Maroon Moment: Rebel Slaves in Early Seventeenth Century Guatemala," *Slavery & Abolition* 25 (December 2004): 44–58.

4. See Richard Price, *The Guiana Maroons: A Historical and Bibliographical Introduction* (Baltimore and London: Johns Hopkins University Press, 1976); Wim Hoogbergen, *The Boni Maroon Wars in Suriname* (Leiden: E. J. Brill, 1990); Richard Price, *To Slay the Hydra: Dutch Colonial Perspectives on the Saramaka Wars* (Ann Arbor, Mich.: Karoma Publishers, 1983); Philippe Fermin, *An Historical and Political View of the Present and Ancient State of the Colony of Surinam in South America* (London: the author, 1781); and Sylvia W. de Groot, "A Comparison between the History of Maroon Communities in Surinam and Jamaica," in *Out of the House of Bondage*, ed. Heuman, 173–84.

5. See Gabriel Debein, "Marronage in the French Caribbean"; and Yvan Debbasch, "Le Maniel: Further Notes"—both in *Maroon Societies*, ed. Price; Laurent Dubois, *Avengers of the New World: The Story of the Haitian Revolution* (Cambridge, Mass.: Harvard University Press, 2004); and Carolyn E. Frick, *The Making of Haiti: The Saint Domingue Revolution from Below* (Knoxville: University of Tennessee Press, 1990). See also Jean Fouchard, *Les marrons de la liberté* (Port-au-Prince: Henri Deschamps, 1988).

6. See Herbert S. Klein, *African Slavery in Latin America and the Caribbean* (Oxford: Oxford University Press, 1986); Stuart B. Schwartz, *Sugar Plantations in the Formation of Brazilian Society: Bahia, 1550–1835* (Cambridge: Cambridge University Press, 1985); and R. K. Kent, "Palmares: An African State in Brazil"; Roger Bastide, "The Other Quilombos"; and Stuart B. Schwartz, "The Mocambo: Slave Resistance in Colonial Bahia"—all three in *Maroon Societies*, ed. Price.

7. See Daniel Lee Schafer, "The Maroons of Jamaica: African Slave Rebels in the Caribbean," Ph.D. diss., University of Minnesota, 1973; Mavis C. Campbell, "Marronage in Jamaica: Its Origin in the Seventeenth Century," in *Comparative Perspectives on Slaves in New World Plantation Societies*, ed. Vera Rubin and Arthur Tuden (New York: New York Academy of Sciences, 1977), 389–419; Orlando Patterson, "Slavery & Slave Revolts: A Sociohistorical Analysis of the First Maroon War 1665–1740," in *Maroon Societies*, ed. Price; and Emilla Viotti da Costa, *Crowns of Glory, Tears of Blood: The Demerara Slave Rebellion of 1823* (Oxford: Oxford University Press, 1994).

8. Quoted in Sally Hadden, *Slave Patrols* (Cambridge, Mass.: Harvard University Press, 2001), 30.

9. Quoted in Allan Kulikoff, *Tobacco and Slaves: The Development of Southern Cultures in the Chesapeake, 1680–1800* (Chapel Hill: University of North Carolina Press, 1986), 328.

10. Richmond paper cited in *Pennsylvania Packet*, July 19, 1787.

11. *William Byrd's Histories of the Dividing Line betwixt Virginia and North Carolina* (New York: Dover Publications, 1967), 56.

12. Johann David Schoepf, *Travels in the Confederation, 1783–84* (Philadelphia: Wm J. Campbell, 1911), 99–100.

13. John Ferdinand Smyth, *A Tour of the United States of America: Containing an Account of the Present Situation of That Country* (Dublin: G. Perrin, 1784), 65.

14. John R. McKivigan, ed., *The Roving Editor, or Talks with Slaves in the Southern States, by James Redpath* (University Park: Pennsylvania State University Press, 1996), 275; Porte Crayon cited in Bland Simpson, *The Great Dismal: A Carolinian's Swamp Memoir* (Chapel Hill: University of North Carolina Press, 1990), 73, 76. Some interesting archaeological evidence suggests late eighteenth- and early nineteenth-century occupation of a drier part of the Dismal Swamp called Culpepper Island. See Elaine Nichols, "No Easy Run to Freedom: Maroons in the Great Dismal Swamp," master's thesis, University of South Carolina, 1988, 119–29. See also Daniel O. Sayers, P. Brendan Burke, and Aaron M. Henry, "The Political Economy of Exile in the Great Dismal Swamp," *Journal of Historical Archaeology* 11 (March 2007): 60–97.

15. Marvin L. Michael Kay and Lorin Lee Cary, *Slavery in North Carolina, 1748–1775* (Chapel Hill: University of North Carolina Press, 1995), 99; petition of Thomas Lucas,

November 25, 1788, North Carolina General Assembly, session records, North Carolina State Archives, Raleigh; *Wilmington City Gazette,* July 18, 1795.

16. See petitions of John Rhem, Terrence Pelletier, William Hill, and John Hill, North Carolina General Assembly, session records, 1822–25, North Carolina State Archives. For more on this episode, see John James Kaiser, "'Masters Determined to Be Masters': The 1821 Insurrectionary Scare in Eastern North Carolina," master's thesis, North Carolina State University, 2006.

17. *Raleigh Register,* March 28, 1811, October 24, 1828; petition of Inhabitants of Sampson, Bladen, New Hanover and Duplin Counties, North Carolina General Assembly, session records, misc. petitions, November 1830–January 1831, North Carolina State Archives; letter to the governor of North Carolina, August 25, 1856, cited in Herbert Aptheker, *American Negro Slave Revolts* (New York: Columbia University Press, 1943), 346; *Wilmington Journal,* August 14, 1856, cited in *New York Herald,* August 19, 1956.

18. Gilbert C. Din, "Cimarrones and the San Malo Band in Spanish Louisiana," *Louisiana History* 21 (Summer 1980): 232–62.

19. *Western Intelligencer* (Ohio), February 6, 1828. For another band in Cypress Swamp near New Orleans, see *Macon Telegraph,* June 30, 1836.

20. *New York Spectator,* July 17, 1827; *Vermont Chronicle,* July 20, 1827.

21. See Jane Landers, "Spanish Sanctuary: Fugitives in Florida, 1687–1790," *Florida Historical Quarterly* 62 (1984): 296–313; Jane Landers, "Gracia Real de Santa Teresa de Mose: A Free Black Town in Spanish Colonial Florida," *American Historical Review* 95 (February 1990): 9–30; and John J. TePaske, "The Fugitive Slave: Intercolonial Rivalry and Spanish Slave Policy, 1687–1764," in *Eighteenth-Century Florida and Its Borderlands,* ed. Samuel Proctor (Gainesville: University Press of Florida, 1975), 1–12.

22. See Nathaniel Millett, "Slave Resistance during the Age of Revolution: The Maroon Community at Prospect Bluff, Spanish Florida," Ph.D. diss., University of Cambridge, 2002.

23. On the Florida maroons and their interaction with the Seminoles, see Kenneth W. Porter, *The Black Seminoles: History of a Freedom-Seeking People* (Gainesville: University Press of Florida, 1996); and Kevin Mulroy, *Freedom on the Border: The Seminole Maroons in Florida, the Indian Territory, Coahuila and Texas* (Lubbock: Texas Tech University Press, 1993).

The Origins of Marronage in South Carolina

CHAPTER ONE

Of all the societies forged by Europeans on the North American mainland, South Carolina quickly became the one most sharply defined by slavery since, unlike Virginia, where slaves only gradually replaced white indentured servants as the dominant form of labor, South Carolina was always intended to be a slave society. Within forty years of the first permanent settlement in 1670 the number of African-born inhabitants was greater than the number of whites, a demographic fact that would persist until the Civil War, and they were almost entirely employed on plantations growing staple crops for export. The fact that South Carolina moved so quickly to become a slave society was due to interlocking factors. First, many of the Lords Proprietors who had invested heavily in the new colony were also members of the Royal African Company, which shipped thousands of Africans to the Americas every year. South Carolina was an obvious new destination for their ships. Second, a large proportion of early settlers in South Carolina came from an increasingly overcrowded Barbados. Barbados had become the most prized British overseas possession due to its sugar exports, and that sugar was grown by imported Africans. Barbadian pioneers in South Carolina brought their own slaves with them and knew exactly what sort of society they desired to create on the mainland. Consequently there was no debate over whether South Carolina would become a slave society and no gradual piecemeal legislation defining what slavery was—everyone knew, and the first slave law in South Carolina, passed in 1690, did not even bother to make clear who was and who was not a slave.[1]

Slavery in South Carolina was a mature system long before the Revolutionary War. During the war, which disrupted life on many plantations, thousands of slaves fled to British lines, and they were eventually evacuated by the British in 1782. Yet plantation slavery was quickly reestablished after 1783. Slavery spread rapidly from its eighteenth-century lowcountry heartland to colonize the midlands and upcountry by the early nineteenth century. It was given added

"An accurate map of North and South Carolina, with their Indian frontier, shewing in a distinct manner all the mountains, rivers, swamps, marshes, bays, creeks, harbours, sandbanks and soundings on the coasts; with the roads and Indian paths; as well as the boundary or provincial lines, the several townships, and other divisions of the land in both the provinces; the whole from actual surveys by Henry Mouzon and others." London: Printed for Robt. Sayer and J. Bennett, 1775. Courtesy of the Library of Congress, Geography and Map Division impetus by the invention in 1793 of the cotton gin, which made growing cotton a commercial reality. New cotton plantations tended to be smaller with fewer slaves than the coastal rice plantations, and this fact inevitably influenced the form that slavery took. Cross-plantation marriages became more common, for instance, but opportunities to visit a city such as Charleston became less frequent.[2] Historians have generally accepted that there were fewer opportunities for remnants of African culture to survive on smaller cotton plantations, compared to those on the larger coastal rice plantations. The smaller numbers of slaves on cotton plantations often lived in close proximity to whites, whereas on the coast, where plantations could be home to several hundred slaves, separate settlements for the enslaved ensured that African linguistic structures, religious beliefs, folk magic, stories, and styles of bodily adornment lingered long into the nineteenth century; these have never entirely disappeared.

Compared to the other significant concentration of slaves in colonial North America in Virginia, more of South Carolina's slave population was African, and they became creolized more slowly. Even in the 1780s about a third of the one hundred thousand slaves in South Carolina had been born in Africa, and this made the state far more like the West Indian islands than the rest of the mainland.[3] Part of the reason for this was that South Carolina continued to import slaves directly from Africa as late as 1807. Although a moratorium had been placed on slave imports between 1787 and 1803, forty thousand new Africans arrived between 1803 and 1807.[4] The ethnicity of South Carolina's slave population has implications for this book. Studies of marronage elsewhere in the Americas suggest that free-born African slaves were more likely to become maroons than native creole slaves were.[5] Africans not only brought with them a determination to regain the freedom that had been taken from them, but they also imported military experience. Several historians have observed, for example, that the use of fortified camps was a common tactic in African warfare, and thus maroons who did the same were simply using their traditional knowledge to defend their settlements.[6]

The size of the African-born population was not the only thing that South Carolina shared with the West Indies. The ratios of white people to slaves were also reminiscent of Caribbean figures: 75 percent of the population of Charleston and Beaufort districts in 1790 were enslaved; by 1830 the proportion of slaves in Charleston District had fallen to 68 percent but risen in Beaufort District to 83 percent, and it had reached 89 percent in Georgetown District.[7] With such a large number of African-born slaves, and so few whites to police them, it was inevitable that some plantations would be completely devoid of white people for large periods of time. Such a combination was extremely conducive to marronage. In these respects South Carolina should perhaps be seen as part of a "greater West Indies" rather than part of the North American mainland, since it clearly shared many more demographic similarities with Barbados and Jamaica than with any other state on the mainland.

Africans working on South Carolina plantations endured harsh, backbreaking labor for twelve hours a day, six (sometimes seven) days a week, and clearing the pine forest was only the start of the job of carving a plantation out of the landscape. The rice culture that quickly became the norm in coastal South Carolina required ditches, drainage channels, and embankments in order to regulate the flow of water. All this came before the annual cycle of planting, hoeing, harvesting, and processing the crop. The work was physically demanding, for both men and women, and was enforced by a system of discipline that emphasized the whip and other punishments for failure to work as overseers and owners directed. The vast majority of African slaves in South Carolina worked on plantations, but a sizable minority lived in Charleston, working as personal or domestic servants for those slaveholders permanently or periodically resident in the provincial capital. The lives of urban slaves were quite different from those of their rural counterparts. In general, urban slaves were better fed and better dressed, but they were also under the close supervision of whites and potentially on call at all hours of the day and night. Nevertheless, urban slaves had greater opportunities to meet and socialize with other slaves, free blacks, and poor whites in the city's numerous churches, bars, and stores. Consequently urban slaves were more likely to be literate and have a greater knowledge of the wider world than field slaves were. One former slave recalled that the best sources of information and news were "Girls that waited on the tables, ladies' maids and the drivers; they would pick up everything they heard and pass it on to the other slaves."[8] Some urban slaves were even permitted to hire their own time, provided they paid their masters a set weekly sum.

Slavery was undoubtedly a varied system. Indeed, its flexibility made it more useful to European settlers, but ultimately it was created and perpetuated by the racist views that white slave owners held of nonwhites. To white eyes, Africans were simple, childlike people with low intelligence, incapable of fending for themselves, and in need of protection from a cruel world. Slavery was defended as the best situation for Africans precisely because it took away their decision-making ability and made them dependent on whites. Planters were able to rationalize their own brutal treatment of enslaved people by claiming that it was impossible to reason with slaves and that they responded best to physical chastisements. Some planters experimented with incentives, such as better food and clothing and more free time, in return for good work, but this was never relied on exclusively. Few slaves avoided the lash for long, and some were beaten extensively and regularly by owners who showed a callous indifference to those they considered property.

Despite the strict regime, those enslaved on South Carolina plantations still managed to create distinct lives for themselves. They married (though not officially), had children, told stories, sang and danced, prayed (though generally not to a Christian God until the nineteenth century), and used spare moments in evenings and on Sundays to grow crops, hunt game, and make handicrafts, which made their lives just slightly more bearable. Nor did most slaves meekly accept their condition of enslavement. They resisted in a variety of active and passive ways, undermining the authority of masters and by doing so proclaiming their own humanity and individuality. Feigning illness, breaking tools, and stealing food were endemic on most plantations, and many slave owners tolerated this to some degree, putting it down to the "stupidity" or innate "depravity" of Africans. Physical resistance was far riskier since even striking a white man could be a capital crime.[9] Yet some slaves still attacked their owners or overseers, either directly or indirectly by using poison. The punishment for poisoning was particularly brutal: in July 1769 "a negroe man and woman were burnt alive on the Green, near the Workhouse, being convicted, one of administering poison, and the other of having procured it."[10] Only rarely did open rebellion occur, most likely because the majority of slaves were aware of its futility in a society with a well-armed and well-organized white militia. The 1739 Stono Rebellion, close to Charleston, was the most singular example of violent slave resistance in South Carolina history. A year later a shaken legislature passed a new act, the Act for the Better Ordering and Governing Negroes. The act banned trading by slaves in Charleston and specifically the sale of alcohol to slaves, restricted the movements of slaves in groups, and proscribed literacy, but in response to suggestions that the Stono Rebellion might have been caused by the lack of restrictions on the power of masters, the new slave law enshrined the right of slaves to Sundays off and to be fed and clothed adequately, and it established punishments for killing slaves. While one might question how much these clauses actually changed the behavior of masters, they are evidence that slaveholders sitting in the legislature recognized that their own treatment of slaves could cause resentment.

That the slave law of 1740 quelled the spirit of resistance among slaves is also doubtful. Insurrection scares continued to rock the state periodically, though concrete evidence of a conspiracy was rarely found. Connecticut-born lawyer Edward Hooker observed the mass panic in Columbia when rumors spread "that a scheme of insurrection has been formed among the negroes on the other side of the river, a few miles above this place, in conjunction with a party below. Their plan is said to be to assault Granby and then come up and burn Columbia; first taking possession of the arms and ammunition deposited in the State House." Within a few hours a field artillery piece had been placed in front of the State House, but while tension remained high throughout the following day, ultimately nothing untoward occurred.[11] South Carolina did not experience another major insurrection scare until 1822, when Denmark Vesey, a free black, was executed, along with thirty-four others, for plotting a rebellion in Charleston. In recent years historians have debated whether Vesey's insurrection was merely in the minds of local whites and not an actual rebellion. The evidence is not completely conclusive, but the balance of probabilities suggests that there was indeed a well-advanced insurrection plot that had spread from its urban roots to encompass some surrounding plantations.[12] As chapter 5 illustrates, Vesey was not the only black man resisting slavery during the 1820s, and while local whites might have been shocked at the scale of his plot, few could claim that slave resistance was unknown in South Carolina. Residents reading Charleston's newspapers with any regularity would have found multiple references to violent and nonviolent acts of resistance committed by slaves.

The failure of Vesey's plot had minimal impact on slavery in the rest of the state. For the remainder of the antebellum era South Carolina's slaves continued to create family ties, worship, and trade in a bewilderingly complex set of environments, but nothing they did undermined the institution of slavery sufficiently to threaten its existence. It would take a civil war to end slavery in South Carolina. This does not mean, of course, that slaves gave up trying to undermine and weaken slavery in numerous ingenious ways. Aside from the passive and active types of resistance mentioned above, which continued unabated, slaves ran away from their masters for varying lengths of time. Between 1732 and 1801 slaveholders advertised for more than two thousand fugitive slaves in South Carolina newspapers, though this was only a small fraction of those who actually ran away since advertising was expensive and many masters hoped, not unreasonably, that fugitives would return voluntarily once hunger became paramount in their minds. Runaways were predominantly young and male and had often been sold several times in South Carolina. Inevitably many fled due to mistreatment, but others tried to return to family and friends.[13] Some struck out for freedom among Indians tribes in the West or the Spanish in Florida or (in the nineteenth century) for the North. An intermediate step was marronage, remaining relatively local to the place of enslavement but with no intention of returning to slavery.

There were differing degrees of marronage in South Carolina. Most common were small groups of up to ten individuals who could be highly mobile, moving between temporary camps and surviving as often by banditry as on their own initiative. Larger groups of up to fifty people were more settled, even engaging in agriculture, and the largest of all, containing up to one hundred maroons, built themselves what might be accurately described as maroon villages with houses surrounded by a defensive palisade. The sizes of maroon groups were not determined only by the number of fugitive slaves, though naturally this was important; they were also dependent on the sizes and locations of the swamp refuges that were easily the most popular locations for marronage in South Carolina. Swamps that were surrounded by plantations could support only relatively small maroon groups partly because it was far more likely that their activities would come to the notice of white people. Raiding surrounding plantations for recruits and supplies often resulted in local whites organizing themselves and attacking maroon camps, eliminating or dispersing the maroons before they became too numerous. Swamps such as those contiguous to the Santee and Savannah rivers were further from the plantation heartlands of South Carolina, and so maroons were far more likely to be able to secrete themselves in places rarely visited by whites and to survive for longer periods of time with minimal impact on local plantations. The longer a maroon group existed, the larger it grew, partly because new runaways were drawn, mothlike, to a successful alternative to plantation life and partly from natural increase. The largest maroon groups differed from the smaller ones by containing both genders and children.

1. David McCord, *The Statutes at Large of South Carolina* (Columbia, S.C.: A. S. Johnson, 1840), 7:343–47.

2. Emily West, *Chains of Love: Slave Couples in Antebellum South Carolina* (Urbana: University of Illinois Press, 2004).

3. Philip D. Morgan, *Slave Counterpoint: Black Culture in the Eighteenth Century Chesapeake and Lowcountry* (Chapel Hill: University of North Carolina Press, 1998), 58–61.

4. Patrick S. Brady, "The Slave Trade and Sectionalism in South Carolina, 1787–1808," *Journal of Southern History* 38 (November 1972): 615.

5. Price, *Guiana Maroons*, 32. This point is also made in Michael P. Johnson, "Runaway Slaves and the Slave Communities in South Carolina, 1799–1830," *William and Mary Quarterly* 38 (July 1981): 419.

6. Sylvia R. Frey, *Water from the Rock: Black Resistance in a Revolutionary Age* (Princeton, N.J.: Princeton University Press, 1991), 52.

7. All population figures are taken from the on-line historical census browser: http://fisher.lib.virginia.edu/collections/stats/histcensus/

8. George Rawick, *The American Slave: A Composite Autobiography*, vol. 3: *South Carolina Narratives* (Westport, Conn.: Greenwood Press, 1973), pt. 5, 52–53.

9. The 1712 slave law stated that minor assaults on whites by slaves would be punished first by whipping, second by branding, and third by death. Inflicting serious injury could lead to an automatic death penalty. See McCord, *Statutes at Large*, 7:359.

10. Report in the *Georgia Gazette*, August 16, 1769. See also Morgan, *Slave Counterpoint*, 613.

11. *Reports of the Historical MSS. Commission of the American Historical Association 1896* (Washington, D.C.: Government Printing Office, 1897), 881–82. For insurrection

scares in Georgetown in 1802, 1810, and 1829, see Charles Joyner, *Down by the Riverside: A South Carolina Slave Community* (Urbana: University of Illinois Press, 1984), 233. See also Norrece T. Jones Jr., *Born a Child of Freedom, Yet a Slave: Mechanisms of Control and Resistance in Antebellum South Carolina* (Hanover and London: Wesleyan University Press, 1990), 182–93.

12. The best summary of the historiographic debate is in Douglas R. Egerton, *He Shall Go Out Free: The Lives of Denmark Vesey*, 2nd ed. (New York: Rowman & Littlefield, 2004), 234–51.

13. Daniel E. Meaders, "South Carolina Fugitives as Viewed through Local Colonial Newspapers with Emphasis on Runaway Notices, 1732–1801," *Journal of Negro History* 60 (April 1975): 288–317.

Document 1.1 is the earliest reference we have to a maroon group in South Carolina. There is no specific information as to where in South Carolina Sebastian, "the Spanish Negro," was located, but it was almost certainly near the coast since white settlement had not spread far inland by 1711.

1.1] *Maroons led by Sebastian, the "Spanish Negro," 1711*[1]

June 20, 1711

The House being inform'd that there are several Negroes runaway from their Masters & keep out, arm'd, robbing & plundering houses & Plantations & putting ye Inhabitants of this province in great fear and terrour.

Revolved, by this house that ye Govern^r be addressed to take effectual care to apprehend take & suppress ye said runaways & to assure his hon^r that this House will at all times be ready to concur wth the Govern^r & Council in defraying the expenses of soe good & necessary a designe.

June 21, 1711

Read an address to ye Govern^r to request him to Issue forth his Commission to prepare psons to apprehend, hunt & take the runaway Negroes & to Employ a number of Indians to assist them (viz).[2]

October 10, 1711

On ye constant complaints since ye last meeting of divers psons of this Province of the Barbarities, Fellonies & abuses committed by some runaway Negroes on our Inhabitants, wee desired such members of yor House as was then in Town to meet us & wee agreed to give unto any person who should take or bring, dead or live, Sebastian the Spanish or fidlings Negroe as an encouragem^t, fifty pounds, & to such as should take up any other Negro runaway forty days, five pounds for the Confirmation whereof we want the Concurrence of yor House & since we are on this subject, do think it a matter worthy of yor highest consideration, immediately to draw up such a Bill for the better ordering of Slaves, that effectively prevent those fears and jealousies wee now lye under from the Insolence of the Negroes we have already in this province & the numbers that are daily brought unto us

Robert Gibbes[3]

October 11, 1711

Ordered. That Richard Berisford Esqr Publick Receiver do pay out of the Publick Treasury unto Eliza Dutch Widd{o} the Sume of Thirty pounds for the reliefe of her selfe & her poor family the said Elizabeth having her House & all her Substance burned by Bastian, the Spanish Negroe who was Lately Executed & that this order be sent to the Govern{r} & Council for their Concurrance.

Ordered. That Richard Berisford Esqr Publick Receiver do pay out of the Publick Treasury unto Sarah Perry Widd{o} the sume of Tenn pounds Curr{t} money in consideration of the great Loss she sustained by the death of her Indian, who was killed by Bastian, the Spanish Negroe, and that this order be sent to the Govern{r} & Council for their Concurrance.

Ordered. That Richard Berisford Esqr Publick Receiver do pay out of the Publick Treasury unto the Indians who took & killed Bastian, the Spanish Negroe, the summe of fifty pounds curr{t} money as a reward for that Publick Service and that this order be sent to the Govern{r} & Council for their Concurrance.

1. Journal of the Commons House of Assembly, 1710–12, South Carolina Archives.
2. Address missing in original.
3. Governor of South Carolina between 1710 and 1712.

As instructed by the governor, the legislature duly passed a new law "for the better ordering and governing of Negroes" in June 1712 in order, they explained, to tame the "wild, savage natures" of those enslaved in South Carolina. New restrictions were placed on the movement and meetings of slaves, and harsher penalties were decreed for crimes committed by slaves: running away, for instance, became a capital crime for the first time. This new regime was unsustainable, partly because too many slaves were being executed and the compensation being paid to owners was draining the public treasury. Therefore, two years later a new slave law was passed introducing an alternative punishment of transportation. This alternative was in turn withdrawn in 1717 out of fear that it actually encouraged slaves to commit crimes in the hope of improving their situations. Slave laws continued to be passed regularly. One in 1722, for example, ordered that slaves be prevented from breeding and owning horses because they were used to "convey secret intelligences from one part of the country to another," but there was no appreciable diminution in maronage.[1] In 1733 the South Carolina legislature heard reports of maroons gathered in the interior of the province "near the Congarees," the Indian tribe that had resided near modern-day Columbia (document 1.2). The swamp on the north side of the Congaree River stretched as far as the confluence with the Wateree and, as later documents show, would prove popular with maroon groups.

1. Cooper, *Statutes at Large*, 7:353–84.

1.2] The South Carolina Upper House of Assembly offers a reward for maroons near the Congarees, 1733[1]

In the Upper House of Assembly Friday ye 14th Sepr 1733

The following message was brought from the Lower House by Maj^r Fitch & Col^o Prioleau vizt

On reading a Letter from Capt Charles Russell to the honble Thomas Broughton[2] Esqr relating to Several Run away negroes who are near the Congarees & have robbed Several of the Inhabitants Thereabouts.

Ordered, That a Reward of £20 p head be paid by the Publick Treasurer to any Person or Persons whatsoever who shall take them a Live & Ten pounds p head for Those who shall be taken dead.

We desire your Excelley will be pleased to take such measures in this Affair, as you Shall think proper, that the end proposed by the above Resolution may not prove Ineffectual.

By order of the house
Paul Jenys Spk^r
14th Sepr 1733

1. Journal of the Upper House of Assembly, 1733, South Carolina Archives.
2. Later governor of South Carolina, 1735–37.

Two years later the governor ordered out the local militia against maroons living on the most northerly of the four tributaries into Charleston harbor, the Wando River.

1.3] The governor orders the militia against maroons on Wando River, 1735[1]

The following Order was delivered to the Provost Marshall.

By the Honble Thos Broughton Esqr Lieut Gov^{or} and Commander in Chief &^{a} of South Carolina.

Whereas I have received Information that Several White persons and Blacks, have committed many Outrages and Robberys and lye in the Swamp at the Head of Wando River, where they bid defiance to the Chief Justice's Warrant by him Granted for the apprehending of them, as well as to the Coll Power, you are therefore directed and required upon application from the Marshal or his Deputy or Deputys to order the Captain of the Company which is nearest those parts, to order so many of his men as shall be judged sufficient to seize and apprehend those disturbers of the Peace, by taking them alive, and causing them to be safely conducted to the Gaol in Charles Town, or in case of resistance from them, to exercise military discipline; either by shooting them or otherwise.

Given under my hand in the Council Chamber the 29th day of May 1735.
Thos Broughton

1. South Carolina Council journal, May 29, 1735, South Carolina Archives.

In 1744 the South Carolina government authorized the use of the Notchee Indians to hunt maroons. While there is no specific location mentioned in the source, the Notchees, remnants of the Natchez tribe that had fled French territory in 1725, were encamped near Four Hole Swamp in Colleton County and in April 1744 had offered their services to Gov. James Glen for precisely this purpose.[1]

1. South Carolina Council journal, September 18, 1738, April 13, 1744, U.K. National Archives, London, CO 5/448, 187–88; Chapman J. Milling, *Red Carolinians* (Chapel Hill: University of North Carolina Press, 1940), 227–28.

1.4] *The South Carolina Council approves the use of Notchee Indians against maroons, 1744*[1]

His Excellcy the Govr acquainted the board, that Captn Richard Wright had applied to him, for the assistance of some Notchee Indians in order to apprehend some runaway Negroes, who had sheltered themselves in the Woods, and being armed, had committed disorders in that neighbourhood.

His Excellency thereupon, wrote the following letter to Mr James Coachman viz
Charles Town July 5th
Mr James Coachman Sir

Captn Richard Wright having informed me that there are some runaway Negroes who shelter themselves in the woods in this Neighbourhood, and having procured arms, comit divers disorders wch may be of evil example, to other negroes, and prove hurtful to the Inhabitants of this province, if not totally taken notice of & suppressed, you are therefore to notify my Good Friend, Will, King of the Notchees, that he send some of his men, to put themselves under the direction, and Command of the sd Capt Richard Wright, and to obey his orders, in all things touching these daunting negroes and as what is done in this matter, by my Friends the Notchees, will be a service to the Province, & it will be a favour done to me, and for their so[l]d[i]ering this Letter shall be a sufficient warrant from &c

James Glen.

1. South Carolina Council journal, July 5, 1744, U.K. National Archives, CO 5/450, 383–84.

Five years before the Notchees came to the aid of the provincial government, a full-fledged slave rebellion had broken out on the banks of the Stono River a short distance south of Charleston. Motivated apparently by offers of freedom from the Spanish in Florida, as well as long-standing resentment about their own treatment by whites, the hundred or so rebels marched in quasi-military style southward, killing and destroying property as they went. Eventually the militia routed the rebels, but the contemporary sources (written in 1739 or immediately afterward) are silent on where the Stono rebels actually came from and how they managed to gather in a significant body and start a rebellion. Gov. William Bull Jr., writing more than thirty years after the event, thought that "too great a number had been very indiscreetly assembled and encamped together for several nights, to do a large work on the public road; with a slack inspection."[1] *If this was really the case, then why did the 1740 Negro Act, passed by the provincial legislature in the aftermath of the rebellion and placing numerous restrictions on the activities of slaves, make no mention of the need for increased vigilance or supervision over road gangs? Of course, Bull's comment cannot be entirely discounted, but it is possible that this was just the most plausible explanation that suggested itself to him at the time he was writing in 1770. Perhaps not all of the Stono rebels were plantation slaves, as has generally been assumed, but instead were augmented by maroons who had fled bondage long ago and, lured by Spanish promises of liberty, were at that point seeking to end the threat of reenslavement by traveling to St. Augustine. Perhaps the involvement of maroons, who did not have to wait for an opportunity to flee from a plantation under the watchful eye of an owner or overseer, explains how the number of rebels grew so quickly, reaching as many as a hundred within a few hours. We cannot know for certain if some of the rebels at Stono had been maroons, but considering that the location for the start of the rebellion—the ignition point—was on the fringes of the Stono Swamp and that (as this book makes clear) maroons were endemic in the swamps, it is not beyond the bounds of probability that they were involved.*

The Stono rebels certainly exhibited some of the traits often associated with maroons: they were armed and well organized; most sought to preserve their liberty, rather than fight to the death, by retreating "to a thicket of woods" after the initial encounter with the militia; and some of those fleeing evidently had the requisite skills to support themselves while hiding from white pursuers. Thirty rebels managed to traverse about thirty miles heading southward before being overtaken by the militia forces and reengaged in battle. Once again the majority of the rebels escaped, and three weeks after the initial revolt John Martin Bolzius, pastor of the Salzburgers at Ebenezer in Georgia, noted that "the Negroes or Moorish slaves are not yet pacified but are roaming in gangs in the Carolina forests."[2] Over the ensuing months it became clear that some of the escaped rebels had become maroons, or perhaps returned to being maroons. In November 1739 the South Carolina Commons House of Assembly ordered regular armed patrols of the Stono region "for their better Security and Defence against those Negroes which were concerned in that Insurrection who are not yet taken."[3] In late 1742, more than three years after the rebellion, the *South Carolina Gazette* noted that "one of the Ringleaders of the last Negro Insurrection (belonging to Mr Henry Williamson) was lately seized in Cotaw Swamp, by two Negro Fellows that ran away from Mr Grimke, who brought him to Stono, where he immediately was hang'd."[4] It is an indication of the ineffectiveness of white patrols that this man was found by other runaway slaves. The two slaves, despite being runaways themselves, were later rewarded by the South Carolina legislature "in the same Manner as other Slaves had been formerly rewarded for apprehending others of the said rebellious Negroes."[5]

In document 1.5 two slaveholders apply for compensation for slaves killed by those in pursuit of maroons near Stono in 1750. It is possible that these maroons had actually participated in the 1739 rebellion and remained hidden in the swamps for more than a decade, though there is no way to prove this. Local Indians were employed alongside the militia to hunt the maroons, as they had been in the immediate aftermath of the Stono Rebellion, killing several.[6] Shortly after this episode of marronage, and perhaps in response to it, the South Carolina legislature increased the punishments for slaves who ran away, making a distinction between ordinary runaways who were absent less than three months and those "Notorious run-away slaves who shall be run-away 12 months." The latter, "which runaway and lie out for a considerable space of time, at length become desperate, and stand upon their defiance with knives, weapons or arms," could be pursued by any white person, and "if such run-away cannot be otherwise taken it shall be lawful to kill such notorious offenders."[7]

1. Mark M. Smith, ed., *Stono: Documenting and Interpreting a Southern Slave Revolt* (Columbia: University of South Carolina Press, 2005), 31.

2. Ibid., 7, 11, 15.

3. J. H. Easterby, *The Journal of the Commons House of Assembly September 12, 1739–March 26, 1740* (Columbia: S.C. Historical Commission, 1952), 37.

4. *South Carolina Gazette*, December 27, 1742. It has not been possible to find Cotaw Swamp on a contemporary map, though conceivably it might be a corruption of Cawcaw Swamp, north of the Stono River.

5. J. H. Easterby, *The Journal of the Commons House of Assembly September 14, 1742– January 27, 1744* (Columbia: S.C. Historical Commission, 1954), 263, March 2, 1743.
6. Easterby, *Journal of the Commons House of Assembly September 12, 1739–March 26, 1740*, 65.
7. R. Nicholas Olsberg, ed., *The Colonial Records of South Carolina: The Journal of the Common House of Assembly, 23 April 1750–31 August 1751* (Columbia: University of South Carolina Press, 1974), 287–88; McCord, *Statutes at Large*, 7:424.

1.5] *Account of John McLeod and petition of William Kelvert, January 28, 1751*[1]

An account of Mr. John McLeod, amounting to the Sum of two hundred & fifty Pounds it being for a Negro Man named Ben, belonging to the said Mr. McLeod that was shot dead by one of the Patrol of Stono District, who were in pursuit of fugitive Slaves. And also a Certificate by Mr. William Butler, the Commander of the said Patrol, That the said Patrol (on the fifteenth Day of June one thousand seven hundred and fifty) being in quest of some Run-away Negroes, did surprise a Camp of them on the Marshes near New-Cut; and firing among them, one of the said Runaways was killed upon the spot; which they were then informed (by some of Mr Grimbald's Negroes) belonged to the reverend Mr. John McLeod; and that his name was Ben. And also a Deposition of Mr. Benjamin Harvey and George Harvey taken before James Bulloch Esqr., one of His Majesty's Justices of the Peace, on the twenty seventh Day of December one thousand seven hundred & fifty, That the Negro mentioned in the said Certificate was (by command of Ensign William Butler) shot dead, at the Place, and on the occasion mentioned by the said Mr. Butler in the said Certificate. And that upon examining of the dead Body (by the information of the other Negros who were taken) it was generally said and believed that he was a Slave belonging to the reverend Mr. John McLeod, and was named Ben; Which Certificate and Deposition were to the said Account annexed.

And then the Petition of William Kelvert of Stono, Planter, to his Excellency the Governor, and His Majesty's hon: Council and this House, was read to the House, setting forth,

"That the Petitioner, with all his Family, have, for a long time, lived and resided on Stono River, and followed the planting Trade, and, at the same time, was possessed of a certain Negro Man Slave named Hector: But it happened that some Disturbance on account of the Run away fugitive Negro Slaves, on which Captain Elisha Butler raised his Company of the Militia, in order to suppress them; and at the same time hired a Gang of Indians for his assistance to scour the Swamps thereabouts for the said fugitive Slaves.

"That the Petitioner's Plantation is adjacent thereunto, and the Petitioner's Slave afore mentioned happening to go some distance from the said Plantation, and in sight of the Inhabitants thereabouts, was met by the said Indians; one of whom shot him that he dyed of his Wounds: as is and can be made appear by a Certificate under the hand of the aforesaid Elisha Butler, Commander of the said Company.

"That the Petitioners said Negro was a hard working Fellow, and always behaved himself as a Slave ought to do; and the Petitioner is at a great Loss for the want of him, not being able to carry on his Plantation business.

"And therefore most humbly praying his Excellency and their Honours to take the case into consideration: and that as the said Indian did kill the said Negro, who had never transgressed the Law, his Excellency and their Honrs. will be pleased to allow him such Satisfaction as the Laws, both of the Militia and the Negro Act in that case made and provided do allow."

Ordered, that the said Petition be referred to the consideration of the Committee who were appointed to examine the several Petitions and Accounts of the Public Debt from the twenty fifth Day of March in the year of our Lord one thousand seven hundred and fifty to the twenty fifth day of March one thousand seven hundred and fifty one; and they are to examine the matter of the said Petition, and to report the same, as it appears to them, with their opinion thereupon to the House.[2]

1. Olsberg, ed., *Colonial Records of South Carolina*, 208–9.
2. McLeod received £125 and Kelvert £200 in compensation, though the House of Assembly was clear that these payments did not set a precedent (ibid., 257).

Documents 1.1 to 1.5 are evidence that marronage in South Carolina can be clearly dated back to the early eighteenth century and that it occurred in several different parts of the province. Chapter 2 deals with major maroon events in the 1760s and early 1770s that were far more extensive and serious than those that had occurred before.

A Late Colonial Burst of Marronage, 1765–1774

CHAPTER TWO

Maroon communities clearly had existed throughout South Carolina from at least the early eighteenth century, but suddenly in 1765 they became much more of a problem for white authorities in South Carolina and especially near the Georgia border. One possible explanation for the timing of this explosion of maroon activity is that the Stamp Act went into operation on November 1, 1765. This attempt by the British government to raise revenue by taxing official documents and publications was the cause of much disagreement between elected assemblies and royally appointed colonial governors throughout the American colonies. The *Georgia Gazette* reported fully on the uproar caused elsewhere by the Stamp Act during September and October 1765, though Georgia's main settlement, Savannah, remained generally calm throughout the dispute due in large part to the diplomacy and level-headedness of Gov. James Wright. Sailors in Savannah did, however, celebrate the anniversary of the Gunpowder Plot on November 5, 1765, by acting out the lynching of a stamp collector, in effect hinting at the violence that might have ensued if Governor Wright had taken a harder line.[1]

In South Carolina the situation was far more volatile. The House of Assembly had sent representatives to the Stamp Act Congress in October 1765, and Lt. Gov. William Bull reported back to London on the "very extraordinary and universal commotions in the town." People in Charleston were evidently resolved to destroy the stamps when they arrived and disrupt the work of the stamp collectors, and indeed the house of one tax inspector in Charleston was badly damaged by a mob.[2] The internal divisions among whites would have been obvious to urban or domestic slaves and could well have encouraged slaves to take advantage of the political instability and flee from bondage. With many masters absent in Charleston and Savannah, either attending sessions of the legislature or concentrating on plotting resistance to the Stamp Act, the Provincial Grand Jury for South Carolina complained that rural slave patrols were not being undertaken regularly and that some plantations were totally devoid of white people.³ In such circumstances it is likely that marronage became easier and indeed that the maroons were emboldened by the lack of unified authority among whites.

1. *Georgia Gazette,* November 7, 1765.
2. Lieutenant Governor Bull to the Board of Trade, November 3, 1765, cited in William Roy Smith, *South Carolina as a Royal Province 1719–1776* (New York: Macmillan, 1903), 351–52; Richard Walsh, *Charleston's Sons of Liberty: A Study of the Artisans, 1763–1789* (Columbia: University of South Carolina Press, 1959), 36.
3. *South Carolina Gazette,* October 31, 1765.

The maroons in the Savannah River region were first mentioned in 1765, located on the north side of the river opposite Savannah. It is not specified how long the maroons had been there, only that "of late" they had been raiding plantations. The estimate of the size of this maroon band at about forty strong fits in well with the evidence since the four houses mentioned in document 2.2 were comparable in size to slave quarters that housed up to ten individuals each (Morgan, Slave Counterpoint, *106–8). The letter of Roderick McIntosh (document 2.2) tells us a great deal about the internal organization of the maroons. Document 2.3 is a request for compensation by a slave owner who lost a slave during the battle with the maroons and is evidence that some enslaved people were used, willingly or unwillingly, against the maroons.*

2.1] *Georgia's House of Assembly acts on information regarding a maroon settlement on the Savannah River, November 15, 1765*[1]

Fryday November 15th 1765

This house having received information upon oath that a number of fugitive slaves belonging to inhabitants of this province have assembled themselves together in the River Swamp on the North Side of the River Savannah from whence they have of late frequently come into the plantations on the South side of the said River and Committed several robberies and depredations. In order therefore to put a stop to such depredations for the future.

Resolved

That this house will provide a sum not exceeding one hundred Pounds Sterling to be distributed and paid by the Treasurer in the following Manner—

That is to say

For every male fugitive slave as aforesaid of the age of sixteen years or upwards found in actual arms or being in company with any that are armed if taken alive and delivered to the warden of the work house within the space of fourteen days from the date hereof the sum of five pounds sterling.

For the head of every such slave making resistance or attempting to escape two pounds sterling—

And for every woman slave as aforesaid or child above the age of five years two pounds sterling.

To be paid by the treasurer to the person or persons demanding the same sufficient proof being first given of such fugitive slave or slaves being taken or killed as aforesaid.

1. Journal of the Commons House of Assembly, 1763–68, in *The Colonial Records of the State of Georgia*, ed. Allen D. Candler (Atlanta: Franklin-Turner, 1907), 14:292–93.

2.2] *Georgia governor James Wright writes to Lt. Gov. William Bull of South Carolina regarding the maroon community on the Savannah River, November 25, 1765* [1]

In the Council Chamber,
Monday the 9th day of Decr 1765
Present
His Honor the Lt Govr
[The Honble Orthniel Beale, Henry Middleton, Thomas Shottowe, Esqrs][2]

His Honor the Lieutenant Governor laid before this board the following Letter which he had this morning received from Governor Wright.
Savannah in Georgia 25th November 1765
Sr

For some time past it has been discovered that a Number of run away Negroes partly belonging to People in this Province, Partly to People in your Province, have got together on the North Side of Savannah River & have frequently in the night time come over on this side killed Cattle and Robbed Several plantations on the South Bank of the River. I have sent partys of the Rangers & of the Militia to search every suspected place, where it was thought run away negroes might take Shelter here but not one Negro or Canoe could be found and altho' it was pretty certain they had taken refuge in your Province, yet I could not get any kind of Proof whereupon to ground any Information to your Honor, till lately the first was the acct given by Mr. Cuthbert's[3] Negroe and the other of Telfair. Upon which I ordered Capt Braddock to go with the Scout Boat & and takg with him a Light rowing Canoe of a proper Size well manned and to watch the mouth of the Creek it was supposed they would Come down, and if possible to apprehend Some of them but unluckily the very night before Braddock was to go Mr. McIntosh unknown to me went in quest of them with a few men which Defeated my Scheeme, for the particulars of Mr. McIntosh's attempt & further information with respect to the number of Negroes &^{ca} I refer to a copy of his Letter and the Inclosed informations which is all the kind of Proof I have been able to get. Mr McIntosh is gone to the Southward, or I could have got his Narrative sworn to, upon the whole Sir if you think proper to give any directions to your Militia on this Occasion, and will Order them to inform me of the precise time and place, when and where they intend to make a Search for these Pernicious Villains I will order some Boats to be on the River and the people to cooperate with yours in their Endeavours to Distroy or rout these Villains.

I have the Honor to be with great reg^d
Sir your most obed^t hble Servt
Ja^s Wright.

And Roderick McIntosh in a letter to Isaac Young Esqr dated Morton Hall the 18th November 1765 informs him that in Consequence of the information given by a Negro fellow belonging to Mr Cuthbert of a Camp of Run away Negroes to the Number of Forty among whom was one Named Ben who belong'd to his Sister Mrs Douglass[4] and whom the said Negro had heard declare his intention of going with a Party to his said Mistresses plantat^n burning her House and killing every white person on the place and also every Negro who should refuse to join him, he had thought it proper to make an attempt on them and accordingly having engaged four white Persons and a free Mulatto named William Martin to accompany him, he had Set out with Mr Cuthbert['s] Fellow for a guide that soon after they met with Two Negroes belonging to Mr Bullock whom they took with them by way of precaution least they should discover them, and proceeded to the Mouth of a Creek past which the Fugitives must pass wch they reached about nine O'Clock at Night that in an Hour thereafter, they Discovered three canoes paddling Softly down the River, That the Negroes discover'd them very Soon afterwards—and upon M^r McIntosh calling to them to Surrender they returned a volley of their arms for an answer, which was returned as Soon as Possible and so Briskly repeated that the Negroes thought it proper to abandon their canoes & Jump into the River. That the Night was Extremely Dark and Foggy which hindered them from Discovering what become of them afterwards but at daylight they found their largest canoe which the Guide informed them was usually man'd by their Head or leading man stopt by an old tree in the River. That on making up to it they found a Quantity of Small Shott a Hatt & Cap with Two Swan Shott through each of them & the sides of the Canoe a good deal smeared with Blood. That on this they were determined to attack their Town, and proceeding up the Creek were hardly got a Quarter of a mile before they discover'd three Negroes whom he supposes at first took them to be of their party and came out to receive a share of their Plunder but on discovering their mistake they betook themselves to the Swamp, that they then proceeded as fast as possible to the Town through the swamp at Least four miles over, and in which they were frequently up to their middle in water & Mudd. That on their coming up to the Town they discovered Two Negroes on a Scaffold one Beating a Drum and the other hoisting of Col[rs], but that on their resolutely coming up they jumpt off the Scaffold and betook themselves to flight after discharging their Guns without doing them any mischief. That on their arrival at the Town, which was then totally deserted they found it a Square Consisting of four Houses seventeen feet long and fourteen feet wide. That the Kettles were upon the Fire boiling Rice and about fifteen Bushels of rough Rice Blankets Potts Pales Shoes Axes and many other Tools, all which together with the Town they set fire too & consumed.

Parish of Christ Church
Savanna

John a Negro fellow belonging to George Cuthbert Esq[r] being examined by me Alexander Wyley one of his Majesty's Justices of the Peace for the Parish of Christ Church declares as follows

That a Negro fellow called Theron belonging also to George Cuthbert Esq[r] told him this Information that about six weeks ago he the said Theron being on the road from the plantation of the Widow Douglass's where he had been sent to work from his Masters Plantation was met by a Negro fellow called Ben belonging to M[rs] Douglass and Two or three other run away negroes. That Ben told Theron he must go with him and not go home as he feared shoud he be permitted to return he would inform that he had seen him which would prevent his being able to get away his wife and Children from his Mistresses Plantation. That Thereon being thereunto compelled he did go with Ben & the other runaway Negroes cross the river Savannah into a creek between the Lands of James Bullock and the Nelville Lands that he went to Head of the said Creek where they all Landed and Walked about four miles in the Woods where there was a camp opposite to a large Savanna in which were many Negroe men, some Women & Children and at least thirty Guns & but little Powder.

That sometime after a party from the said Camp went to the Plantation of Champion Williamson & killed a Beef wch was carried into the Camp. That the said Thereon had afterwards been frequently compelled to go with Partys who were sent out to kill Kattle, and that last night he was with a party of Negroes from the said Camp to the plantation of Lachlan McGillivray Esq[r] where they also killed a Beef that he was Ordered to Carry one Quarter of it down to their Boat which he did but not being immediately followed by any of the other Negroes he made his Escape from them which he had long waited a Good

Opportunity to do, but had until then been afraid to attempt for fear of being killed should he be Discovered, as the Negroe Ben had sometime before shott a fellow named Cork who also belonged to Mrs Douglass for saying he wanted to go home.

The foregoing information was given to me this 12th day of Novr 1765.
Alex Wylly

His Honor thereupon informed the Board that he proposed to give Orders to Col^o Thomas Middleton, who commanded the Militia of Granville County to send out parties of the Militia and if Possible to prevail on some of the Indians in the Settlements to accompany them and to give directions to settle with Governor Wright a Plan for to endeavour to Hunt out & disperse those Nest of Villains & to cooperate with the Partys he should send out for the purpose.

1. South Carolina Council journal, U.K. National Archives, CO 5/486, 43–50.
2. The copy of the council journal in the South Carolina Archives notes those members also present.
3. The Cuthbert plantation was on the Savannah River halfway between Savannah and Ebenezer.
4. This plantation was a few miles south of the Cuthbert plantation on the Savannah River.

2.3] *Archibald Bullock seeks compensation for a slave killed*[1]

February 4, 1766

A petition of Archibald Bullock Gentleman was presented to the House and read setting forth that in the Skirmish with the Runaway Negroes the Petitioner had a Negro Fellow named Colly killed by them to his great Loss and Damage and therefore prays this Honorable House to take the Circumstances of the Case under Consideration and grant him Relief therein.

ORDERED That the said Petition do lie upon the Table for the Perusal of the Members of this House.

1. Journal of the Commons House of Assembly, 1763–68, 347.

The following set of documents details the official response by the provincial government of South Carolina to a large gathering of runaway slaves in Colleton County in late 1765 and early 1766. This part of Colleton County is a flat plain between thirty and fifty miles south of Charleston crossed by many small rivers and three large ones: the Ashepoo, the Combahee, and the Edisto. The geography has always dictated human occupation in the area: the few roads that existed in the colonial and antebellum eras were frequently made impassible by floods that washed away bridges,

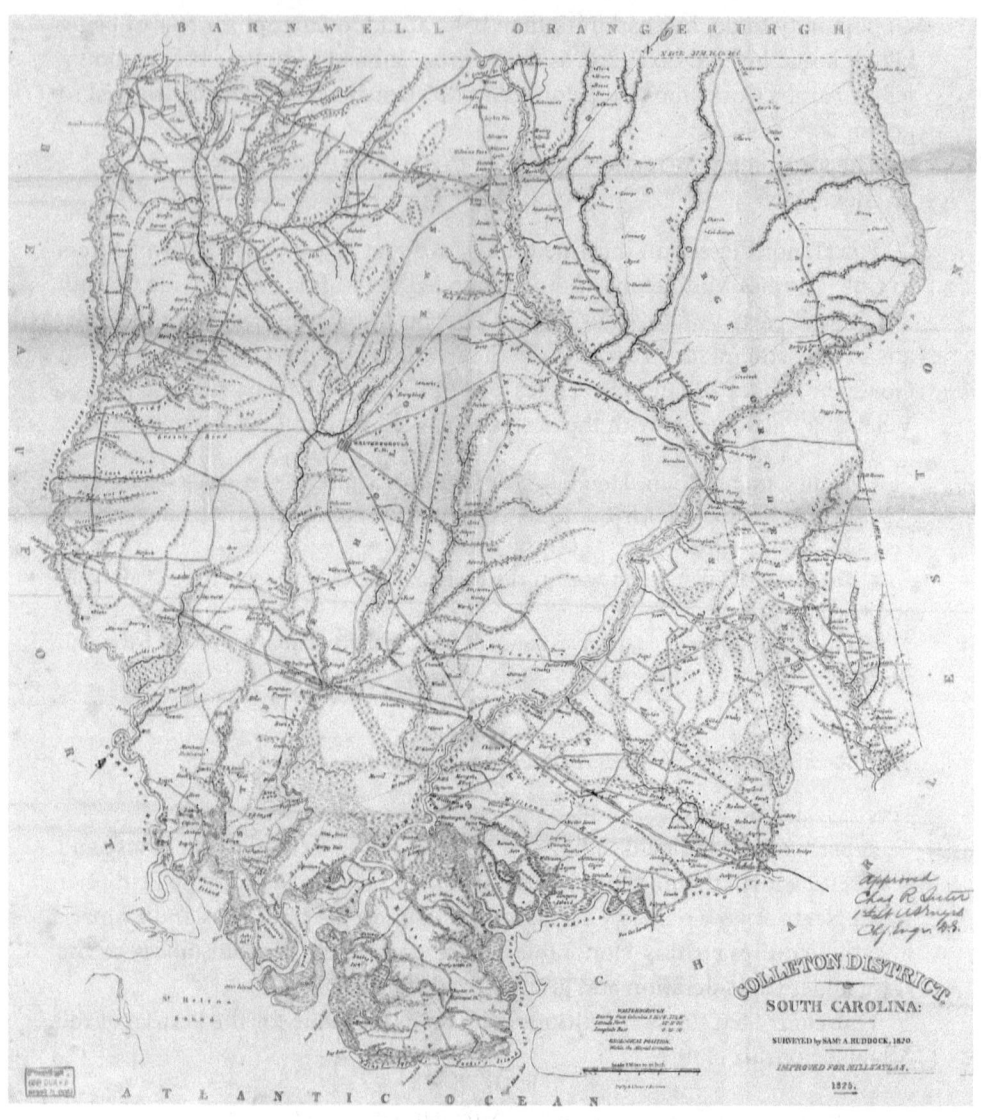

Colleton District, South Carolina, surveyed by Saml. A. Ruddock, 1820; improved for *Mills' Atlas*, 1825. Baltimore: Lucas, 1825. Courtesy of the Library of Congress, Geography and Map Division

so consequently the rivers, and the Atlantic, acted as the main thoroughfares. Even today the main road from Charleston to Beaufort skirts north of this basin. It was well settled by white people in the mid-eighteenth century, though it was not as densely populated as the Ashley and Cooper river regions near Charleston.

The one hundred or so runaways mentioned in document 2.5 joined an already existing "large number" of maroons, making this one of the largest incidences of marronage in South Carolina. There are several interesting points to consider. Lt. Gov. William Bull evidently conflates marronage and insurrection, and his response is to some extent dictated by his concerns about a rebellion among the large black majority in South Carolina. The "information" he refers to had come initially from the wife of Isaac Huger, who had overheard two slaves discussing "a design of the Negroes to make a Gen[l] insurrection and Massacre of the white People on the night Proceeding Christmas day," and was later apparently confirmed "through Friendship to the White people by two Negroes on John Island."[1] The use of the Catawba Indians as professional "slave catchers" is particularly interesting. Some of the Notchees (see document 1.4) had settled among the Catawba during the 1740s and perhaps had encouraged them to adopt this role.

1. South Carolina Council journal, December 17, 1765, U.K. National Archives, CO 5/486, 55–56.

2.4] **Lt. Gov. William Bull reports to the Board of Trade, Charleston, December 17, 1765**[1]

I cannot forbear observing to your Lordships that the indulgence equitably intended to be given to the British merchants trading to Africa (lest too short a period might have interfered with their adventures) by the Act of Assembly for prohibiting the importation of Negros for 3 years, has in great measure defeated the Salutary End proposed, as above 8000 have been imported this Year, being nearly equal to three Years Importation. Whether this sudden Addition to a number already beyond a prudent proportion will be productive of unhappy consequences, cannot be certainly foreseen, but I have a few days ago reced Intimation that some Plots are forming & some attempts of Insurrection to be made during these Holydays, at which Time slaves are allowed some days of festivity & exemption from labour. I shall therefore take proper measures to prevent the execution of such Designs by giving necessary directions to the Militia & Patrols to be alert of their Duty on that season which I hope will either discourage or suppress their attempt.

1. U.K. National Archives, CO 5/378, 31r/v.

2.5] *The South Carolina Commons House of Assembly debates action against a maroon community in Colleton County, 1766*[1]

January 14, 1766
A message from His Honor the Lt Governor, by the Master in Chancery.
(Viz[t])
Mr Speaker & Gentlemen

During your Recess a little before Christmas, I received some information which appeared to be confirmed by various Circumstances that the Negroes had been forming some scheme for a general Insurrection in this Province to have been put in Execution as on last Christmas day. Whereupon I gave immediate orders for availing ourselves of all the Precautions which the Militia and Patrol laws enable me to take for our security, which were performed with so much alertness throughout the Province, as effectually disappointed all hopes which might have encouraged the Negroes to such an undertaking, and has secured our Quiet and tranquility for the present.[2]

As I had received accounts that one hundred and seven Negroes had left their Plantations soon after the intended Insurrection had been discovered, and joined a large Number of runaways in Colleton County, which might encrease to a formidable Body, I thought it very advisable to call down some of the Catawbas, as Indians strike terrour into the Negroes, and the Indians manner of hunting render them more sagacious in tracking and expert in finding out the hidden recesses, where the runaways conceal themselves from the usual searches of the English, and also that the Negroes may see that Indians are easily to be brought down upon them; I communicated this matter to His Majesty's Council, who advised me to take the measure and I accordingly sent orders to Mr Wyly.[3]

That you may see how far I am engaged, I send for your perusal a copy of my Letter to Mr Wyley and to Col⁰ Jackson. I hope you will Concur with me in the propriety of the measure, and provide for any expence attending it, desiring at the same time your advice in any thing which may render it more effectual.

Several Negroes have been charged with being concerned in planning or promoting the intended Insurrection, they were apprehended this occasioned a very long examination and some expence, which I desire you will make Provision for likewise.

Gentlemen, I cannot leave this subject without observing to you that altho' the late wicked Machinations are now happily disappointed, and seem to be at an end. It is the part of wise men, and will therefore be your care, not to suffer a present appearance of tranquility to lull you into a dangerous neglect of those means upon which only under God, our safety and internal security is established, and to be preserved. The Cause of our Danger is Domestic and interwoven with almost all the Employment of our lives, and so ought to be our attention to the Remedy.

From these considerations I earnestly recommend to you to revise the Militia, Patrol and Town Watch acts and the Acts for better Governing Negroes that such parts as are defective in them may be effectually amended; and most particularly that some method may be established that will enforce not only a punctual but a Continued observance of their Salutary Injunctions.

14th January 1766 William Bull

The Master in Chancery delivered coppy of a Letter from the Lieutennant Governor to Samuel Wyley Esqr, and an other from His honor to Colo Jackson which was read and is as follows:[4]

Charlestown Decemr 25. 1765
Sir,

From several late circumstances and reports there appears some reasons to apprehend that the Negroes about that time intended an Insurrection which might have proved very dangerous if it had taken effect and as a good deal disturbed the Tranquility and alarmed the minds of the people—

To prevent as far as possible any attempts of the like nature for the future it is Judged very necessary to hunt out the Recesses where the runaway negroes harbour as they are the sources from whence such an Evil is most likely to spring, and to effect which no method affords so probably a prospect of success as by employing a party of the Catawba Indians to go upon that service—

I therefore by the advice of His Majestys Council, desire that you will assemble them together and deliver a talk to them in my name informing them, that I do invite them to go upon that service with assurances of a reward for every Run away negro they either apprehend or distroy.—

The spot I have first in View is on both sides of Edisto River, and as many as are willing to go in such an undertaking you will direct them to proceed to Major Glovers near Pon Pon,[5] whom I shall previously furnish with necessary directions for their operations, and as the inclemency of the weather may require it, each of them may be furnished at Kershaw's with a Blanket a pound of powder and flints for which the public will provide. I am persuaded you will use your Endeavours to forward a Service which may be very beneficial to the province. I am &a Sign'd Wm Bull

To Samuel Wyley Esqr
P.S. A party from 10 to 25 will be Enough.

December 30th 1765
Sir

By the death of Coll⁰ Bidon I have appointed you to be Col⁰ and Major Glover to be Lieut Col⁰ of the Colleton County Regiment. I sent the Commission inclosed. I desire you to acquaint me who is the Eldest Captain in your Regiment that I may appoint him to be Major, and also you are to let me know what Commissions are vacant, that they may be filled up as it is impossible that the militia duty can be so well performed as it ought unless all the officers are appointed, and them some of the most ready and active men. Our late alarm shows us how necessary it is, that we should not neglect it.

As is very probable the large number of negroes, said to be run'd away and assembled in the great Swamps near Horses's Shoe,[6] and near Spoons Savanna may give some kind of encouragement to others badly or idly inclined to think of a General Insurrection since the common patrols and such parties of the militia as the Justices and the Commissioned officers by law have power and are directed to send out for the apprehending them, have not been tried at least with any effect, I thought it proper and with the advice of His Majestys Council have sent for a party of the Catawbas from 10 to about 25 with orders to proceed to Major Glover's and for their encouragement, they are to have ammunition and each a Blanket from Mr Kershaw's Store at Pinetree,[7] you are therefore to endeavour before their arrival to prevail on 10 to 15 brisk young men to join the Indians, that they may do no harm by mistaking negroes who are not run away and to spirit them on in their hunting out the negro camps, they may depend on a reward of £30 for every one they take alive, and if any resist the sum of £15 for any one who is killed in such manner upon certificate of any officer or 3 other white men in company with them of the number killed or taken with the master's names, I persuade myself that the Gentlemen who join them and for whose benefit they come down will not desire any part of the reward; if the Indians come you are to consult with Lieut Col⁰ Glover the most effectual measures for apprehending and breaking up these dangerous knots of runaways by hunting thro' the great swamps in St Paul's, as well as St Bartholomew's Parish, very diligently, and send me an account of any discoveries of arms hidden by negroes, which is to be founded, not on report, but certain inquiry, and also of the number of negroes that are now run away which number may be collected from the Several Masters and overseers of Plantations.

I am &c Wᵐ Bull

To Col⁰ George Jackson.
Ordered
That the said Message and Letters be taken into Consideration tomorrow morning.

Wednesday 15th day of January 1766

The House proceeded to take into consideration the Lieut governors message of the 14th instant.

Upon reading the 1st 2d & 3d paragraphs thereof, and copies of the Lieut governor's letter to Mr Wyley and Colo Jackson.

Resolved

That this House doth approve of the steps taken by His Honor the Lieut Governor and his majesty's Council upon the late Rumour of an insurrection amongst the Negroes.

Resolved

That this House will defray the expence of furnishing the Catawba Indians sent for by the Lieut Governor with Blankets, powder and flints.

Resolved

That this House will provide a sum, not exceeding £40 Currency per month for an officer and £30 Currency per Month for a number of men, not more than fifteen to go with the said Indians for three months, if their service shall be so long necessary, such white men providing themselves with arms and ammunition.

Resolved

That this House will provide the sum of thirty pounds Currency for every runaway Negroe the Indians shall take alive and fifteen currency for everyone which they shall kill.

Upon reading the fourth Paragraph of the said Message.

Resolved That this House will provide for defraying the Expence of the confinement and examination of the Negroes mentioned in the said Message when the accounts shall be laid before this House.

Resolved that in case any Negroes shall be killed by the said party of White People and Indians, this House will reimburse the Owners, for the Loss of their Slaves, such sum not exceeding Two hundred Pounds Currency as shall be ascertained to by the Appraisement of three freeholders.

Upon reading the two last paragraphs of the said Message.

Ordered that a Committee of the following Gentlemen be appointed to Revise the Militia, Patrol, and Town Watch Acts, for the better Governing of Negroes, that such parts as are defective in them may be effectually amended.[8]

Mr Pinckney
Mr Parsons
Captn Lampriere
Mr Ben Simons
Mr Parker
Mr Sanders
Mr Clegg

Mr Moultrie
Captⁿ Roper
Mr Dart
Mr Scott
Mr Horry
Mr Cordes

Ordered that a Message be prepared to be sent to his Honor the Lieutenant Governor to inform him of the above Resolutions.

Fryday the 31 January 1766[9]

Ordered that a Committee be appointed to inquire whether there was any Just Grounds for the late report of an Insurrection among the Negroes, and that they do Report there opinion thereupon to the House and what steps are proper to be taken to prevent the like attempts for the future.

Mr Lynch
Mr Legare
Capt Simons
Mr Horry
Mr Dart
Capt Gadsden
Mr Fraser

Ordered that the said Committee have power to send for Persons, Papers, and Records.[10]

Fryday the 28 February 1766[11]

A Message from His Honor the Lieut Governor by the Clerk of the Council viz. Mr Speaker, Gentlemen

I have received a Letter from Col^o Jackson, by King Fron of the Catawba and two others of the party who on my Invitation Came down to hunt out the Runaway Negroes, and Certificates of their having taken seven of them they are now waiting in town for the reward promised them for that service, and desire you will make provision for the same.

27 February 1766   Wm Bull

Ordered

That the public Treasurer do advance to His Honor the Lieut Governor a sume not exceeding £210 Currency to pay the Catawba Indians for taking Seven Runaway Negroes.

Ordered

That the public Treasurer do advance a further sume not exceeding £230 Currency to His Honor the Lieut Governor to be laid out in presents for the said Indians.

Saturday the 15 March 1766[12]
   Another message from His Honor the Lieut Governor
   Mr Speaker & Gentlemen
   Yesterday afternoon I received by the hands of some Catawba's the Letter from Colo Jackson & certificate from Capt Stephens herewith sent for your Perusal, signifying that nine Runaway Negroes had been taken since King Fron came to town from Ponpon seven of whom were taken by the Catawba's. I desire you to make provision for the payment of such as have been taken agreable to your Resolutions.—It appears by Collo Jackson's Letter that these Catawba's desire only the Head money, being satisfied with the share of Extra presents given their people in Town, while King Fron was in town. I sent orders to Colo Jackson to disband Capt Stevens's Company, and sent back the nine Catawba's from ponpon, but the bad weather prevented his Executing the orders immediately.
   15 March 1766   Wm Bull
   According to order the following message was prepared (viz.)
   May it please your Honor
   . . . in respect to your Honor's recent message just now received, we are to acquaint you that it appears by a Certificate of Capt Stevens that the Catawba Indians have taken only five runaway Negroes, we have therefore resolved to provide £150 for that service.

Wednesday the 9 April 1766[13]
A message from His Honor the Lieut Governor by the Clerk of the Council viz
Mr Speaker & Gentlemen
   I herewith send you the muster scroll of the whitemen, Employed in conjunction with the Catawba Indians, in hunting out the runaway Negroes in Colleton County this winter, together with the account for subsisting the Catawba Indians, that provision may be made for the same.
April 9 1766   Wm Bull

Fryday the 6 of June 1766[14]
   Accounts
   Jacob Stevens for his pay as Captain and also for the pay of thirteen private men under his Command, on a Scout with the Catawba Indians, ordered out by the Lieut Governor in the pursuit of runaway Negroe's vizt.
   To Capt Stevens 1 mo 6 days pay from 5 February to 10th march last inclusive at £40 per mo £48
   To 13 men for their pay the same time at £20 per mo £312
   £360 alld
   Jacob Stevens Senr his account for provisions and sundry necessarys for the Catawba indians who attended him on a scout £140.19: -

Altho this charge is made since 31 December last, yet in the present instance the Committee recommend the same to be provided for.

1. South Carolina Commons House of Assembly journals, U.K. National Archives, CO 5/488, 2–4.
2. Bull ordered regular patrols, especially in and around Charleston, and enlisted the assistance of visiting sailors to police the wharves. See council journal, U.K. National Archives, CO 5/486, 57–58.
3. This was noted in the council journal of December 25, 1765, U.K. National Archives, CO 5/486, 59.
4. These letters are omitted in the copy in the South Carolina Archives but are included in the copy sent to London and now in the U.K. National Archives.
5. Just west of Jacksonborough in Colleton District.
6. Horse Shoe Creek is west of Jacksonborough in St. Bartholomew's Parish and flows into the Ashepoo River.
7. An early name for Camden, South Carolina, on the Wateree River.
8. No changes to any of these laws were made in 1766.
9. South Carolina Commons House of Assembly journals, U.K. National Archives, CO 5/488, 23.
10. This committee never reported.
11. South Carolina Commons House of Assembly journals, U.K. National Archives, CO 5/488, 37.
12. Ibid., 45–46.
13. Ibid., 48.
14. Ibid., 95.

During and immediately after the crisis several contemporaries passed comment on the fear of a full-scale slave insurrection. Compare the comments an anonymous correspondent published in a Boston newspaper (document 2.6) with those of leading planter and politician Henry Laurens (document 2.7) and those of Lt. Gov. William Bull to the Board of Trade in London (document 2.8). The report of the commission on the boundary between North and South Carolina (document 2.9) gives further evidence as to the role played by the Catawba in suppressing the maroons.

2.6] *A resident reports on the scare*

Extract of a letter from South-Carolina, Dec. 29.[1]

"This place has been in an uproar for 12 days past, in consequence of a report which prevailed that the Negroes had agreed to begin a general insurrection throughout the province, and a general massacre was to have began on Christmas eve; it was a happy discovery; circumstances appear very strong. In a little time I expect hanging, gibbeting, burning and whipping without end. Every company in town mount guard day and night."

1. *Boston Evening Post,* February 10, 1766.

2.7] Henry Laurens writes to John Lewis Gervais, January 19, 1766[1]

That disturbance you heard of among our Negroes gave vast trouble throughout the province. Patrols were riding day & Night to 10 or 14 days in most bitter weather & here in Town all were Soldiers in Arms for more than a Week, but there was Little or no cause for all that bustle, some Negroes had mimick'd their betters in crying out "Liberty" & these latter I do believe were apprehensive of an Odious Load falling upon their Shoulders & therefore some of them might probably frame & others propagate Reports to stimulate White Men to Watchfulness in order to prevent any evil consequences but the whole seems to have terminated in the banishment of one fellow, not because he was guilty or instigator of insurrection, but because some of his judges said that in the general course of his Life he had been a sad Dog, & perhaps that it was necessary to save appearances.

1. George C. Rogers Jr., David R. Chesnutt, and Peggy J. Clark et al., eds., *The Papers of Henry Laurens* (Columbia: University of South Carolina Press, 1976), 5:53–54.

2.8] Lt. Gov. William Bull to the Board of Trade, Charleston, January 25, 1766[1]

I have the pleasure to acquaint your Lordships that the apprehensions of a Negro Insurrection last December happily proved abortive. The vigorous execution of our Militia & Patrol laws for 14 days before and after Christmas Day prevented the festivity and Assembling of the Negroes usual at that Time, and disconcerted their Schemes. But as there are several large Parties of Runaways still concealed in large Swamps, not easily accessible by the ordinary way of performing the Patrol duty, I have caused 47 Catawba Indians to come down, whose manner of hunting renders them very sagacious in finding an Enemy by their Track, and who are a terrour to our Negroes, to penetrate into these difficult recesses and kill take or disperse them. That the Indians may not by mistake do wrong to any innocent Negro, they are to be joined by a Party of very alert White Men in the Pay of the Province in this Service. I hope the appearance of these Indians will strike an awe upon the bold Negroes who may incline to form any such destructive Schemes, & discourage such thoughts in them for the future.

1. U.K. National Archives, CO 5/378, 54v/55r.

2.9] *Committee report on the boundary between South and North Carolina*[1]

The staple Commodities of South Carolina being Rice Indico and Naval stores and late Hemp not rivelling or interfering with the produce of Great Britain but being very advantageous to the Trade thereof it is humbly hoped whatever may tend to secure and promote the raising such beneficial Staples must merit the Royal attention. These kinds of produce cannot be raised and extended but by the labour of Slaves supplied by the African Trade which is also very beneficial to Great Britain. But the number of such laborers their condition of slavery being apt to raise in them Ideas of an Interest opposite to their Master becomes dangerous to the publick safety where the number of White Men is overbalanced by a superior number of Negroes wherefore it has been the Policy of South Carolina at great charge to give encouragement to the Importation of Europeans as a Counterpoise thereto, this measure tho very constantly pursued has not been adequate to the growing evil which is the natural consequence of the growing prosperity of the Province. It is therefore very expedient to include in this Province all those Settlers who live on Rivers whose Streams arise to the Westward line of 1764 down which the Hemp Flour and Lumber begin to be brought to Markett at Charles Town, at a less expensive carriage than the present general means of wagons. Bounties are given by South Carolina to Hemp raised in this Province and many living North of where the West Line proposed by Governor Tryon have received our Bounties accordingly and it is but justice to mention the readiness which many of the back settlers expressed to have marched down to assist in suppressing the general Insurrection of our Negroes which was apprehended in 1766, and here let it be remembered that North Carolina is secure from this danger of Negroes for the White men are vastly superior to the Number of Slaves in that Province.

... It would be convenient and reasonable that the Catawba Ind^{ns} should be comprehended in the proposed Boundary as a very useful body of men to keep our negroes in some awe. The year 1766 afforded a very strong proof of their Utility on such services for about Christmas 1765 many Negroes having fled into large swamps and other circumstances concurring there was great room to apprehend that some dangerous conspiracy and Insurrection was intended and tho' the Militia was ordered on duty and were very alert on this occasion the Governor thought it right to invite a number of the Catawba Indians to come down and hunt the Negroes in their different recesses almost impervious to White people at that season of the year the Indians immediately came down and partly by the terror of their name their diligence and singular sagacity in pursuing enemies thro' such thickets soon dispersed the runaway Negroes apprehended several and most of the rest of them chose to surrender themselves to their masters and return to their duty rather than expose themselves to the attack of an Enemy so dreaded and so difficult to be resisted or evaded for which good service the Indians were amply rewarded.

1. South Carolina Council journal, April 4, 1769, 32:145–46, South Carolina Archives.

By 1771 maroons near the Georgia border had shifted from the north side of the Savannah River to the river islands upstream from Savannah. The Savannah River formed the boundary between South Carolina and Georgia and had numerous channels as it neared the sea. The exact demarcation of authority over the marshlands and islands near the river was unclear, and it was not until the Treaty of Beaufort in 1787 that South Carolina and Georgia came to an agreement on the boundary line.[1] *The islands created by the river and the swamps on both sides of it were regularly inundated in the spring, though it is likely that small areas remained dry.*

1. The Treaty of Beaufort was signed on April 28, 1787, and reported in the *Gazette of the State of Georgia*, May 3, 1787. See also Louis De Vorsey, *The Georgia–South Carolina Boundary: A Problem in Historical Geography* (Athens: University of Georgia Press, 1982).

2.10] *Georgia government takes action against a maroon community, December 4, 1771*[1]

At a Council held in the Council Chamber at Savannah on Wednesday the 4th decr 1771
Present
The Honourable James Habersham Esqr
The Honble
Noble Jones
James Mackay
James Edwd Powell
Clement Martin
Lewis Johnson
John Graham
James Read
Esquires

His Honour Acquainted the Board that he had received information that a great number of fugitive Negroes had Committed many Robberies and insults between this town and Ebenezer and that their Numbers (which) were now Considerable might be expected to increase daily: that it appeared absolutely necessary to fall upon Some Spirited measures to take and disperse them to prevent further Inconvenience—

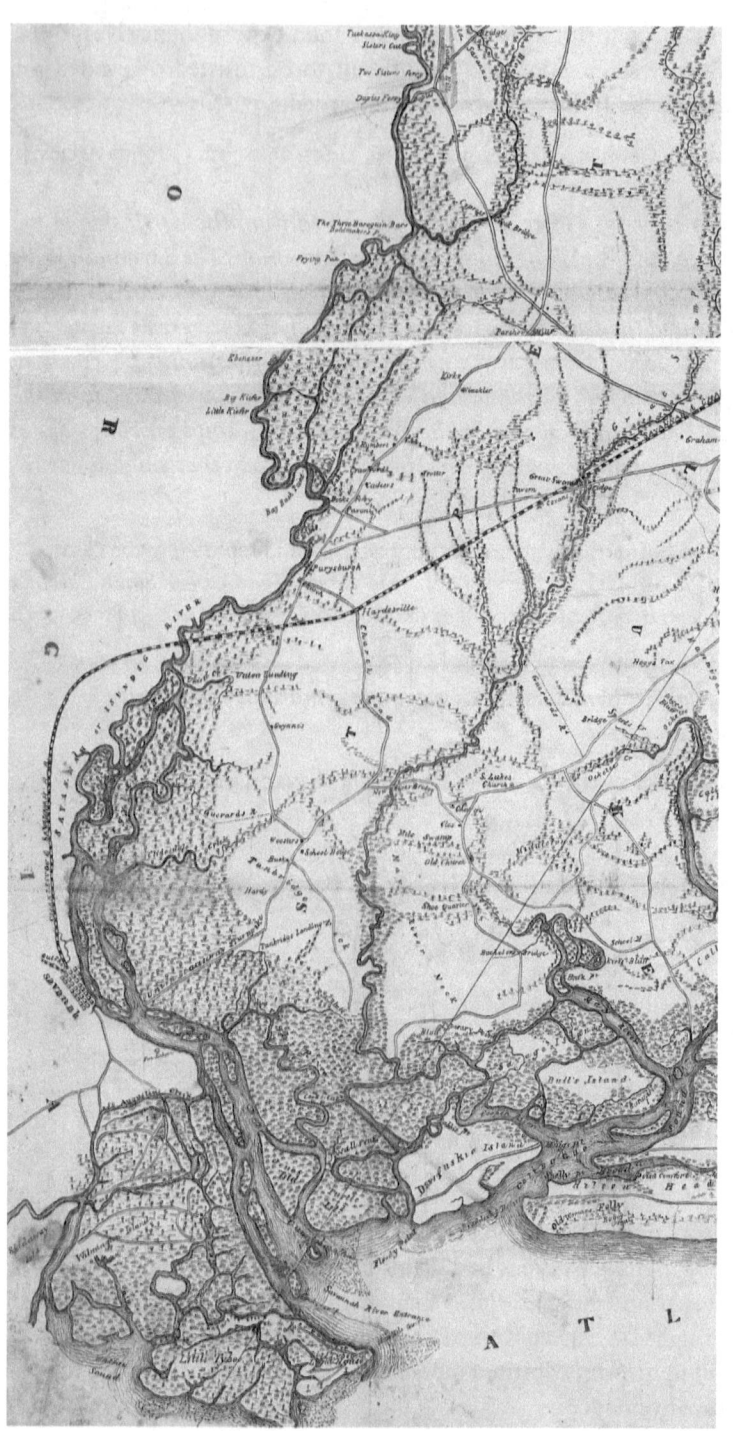

The Board Accordingly took the Same into Consideration and Such parts of the Militia, Patrol and Negro Laws as respected this Matter being read the Board advised his honor to get Mr Moses Nunes (the Indian Interpreter) to engage some Indians to go out that way hunting, in order to discover the Camps of the Negroes and when they had so done to Report the Same, and in that Case to order Capt Wylly with part of the Company of the Militia under his Command to go in Search of and apprehend them and to empower him to give a Small Reward to the said Militia if any Extraordinary duty should be required of them on this necessary Service the Expence of which to be defray'd by the Treasurer by order of his Honor.

His Honor further Observed, that as great numbers of Negroes might be expected in Savannah the ensuing holiday he thought the town Watch insufficient to preserve due order therein and desired the Opinion of the Board what ought or Could be done, to prevent any disorders that might be apprehended—

The Board took the Same into Consideration and Advised his Honor to order Col^l Delegal of the first Regiment of foot Militia to Cause a Patrol duty to be done by the Inhabitants of the said Town and Hamlets, from Tuesday evening preceding Christmas day, until Monday Morning following and that he also gave it in Charge to the Officers of the Watch Company to be Strictly Attentive to have the duty done required of them.

1. Proceedings and Minutes of the Governor and Council, December 4, 1771, in *Colonial Records of the State of Georgia*, ed. Candler, 12:146–47.

2.11] *Georgia's Provincial Grand Jury complains of the activities of runaway slaves, June 1772*[1]

The Presentments of the Grand Jury made at June Sessions was read & it appearing thereby That a number of fugitive Slaves have Assembled themselves on or near the borders of the River Savannah & are frequently committing Depredations on the inhabitants in that Neighbourhood with Impunity & The Board being also informed that the said fugitive Slaves did lately Set fire to a Dwelling house near Black Creek[2] in which a white Child was Burnt to death & also that some Slaves had lately Stopt a boat belonging to Jno Stirk upon the river & taken several articles of Value therefrom, also that some Slaves being at a Camp near Augustins Creek[3] being Surprized by One Fendin a White Man did fire at the said Fendin.

FACING: Beaufort District, South Carolina, surveyed by C. Vignoles and H. Ravenel, 1820; improved for *Mills' Atlas*, 1825. Baltimore: Lucas, 1825. Courtesy of the Library of Congress, Geography and Map Division

And the board takeing the several Circumstances into Consideration Unanimously advised his Honor to direct the Officer Commanding the Company of Militia belonging to the first North West Division to send out Patrols of Men from the said Company In Quest of the said fugitive Slaves on the Main or on the Islands in the River within the patrol Division of the said Comp^y & also that his Honor will order the Commander of the Scout boat to goe up the river Savannah and Search the Creeks & Secret places on the River & Islands as farr as Abercorn Creek in Order to discover & take any of the said fugitive Slaves or their boats.

1. Proceedings and Minutes of the Governor in Council, July 7, 1772, in *Colonial Records of the State of Georgia*, ed. Candler, 12:325–26.
2. On the Georgia side of the river opposite Onslow Island.
3. Also on the Georgia side, opposite Argyle Island, south of Black Creek.

2.12] *The Grand Jury of Beaufort, South Carolina, suggests why maroons were an increasing nuisance*[1]

There is no place of confinement for fugitive slaves in the district and that the gaoler in this district will not take into confinement any such slaves brought to him, and that for want of such a place many slaves are suffered to keep out and do much mischief to the great injury of their owners and others as the Distance to Charlestown's workhouse is so great that when they are taken the captors choose to let them go rather than bear the trouble of delivering them at so great a distance.

1. *South Carolina Gazette*, December 17, 1772.

Periodically local newspapers carried reports of runaway camps that also contained information about the internal organization of maroon communities and how maroons survived when surrounded by large plantations. The 1774 report of the execution of one maroon leader provides a detailed history of his career of crime but also comments on relationships among maroons and, in particular, on maroons' mobility. This maroon camp was near the Beach Hill Meeting House, between the Edisto and the Ashley rivers in St. Paul's Parish, and close to Stono Swamp, which had been popular with maroons before (see document 1.5). Map 4 shows that this location provided ready access to both river systems. Drayton Hall is on the Ashley River.

2.13] *Newspaper report on the capture and execution of Caesar, 1774*[1]

On Tuesday last Week was tried and convicted and executed at Ashley Ferry, that notorious Offender Caesar, a Negro man slave the property of Mr Daniel

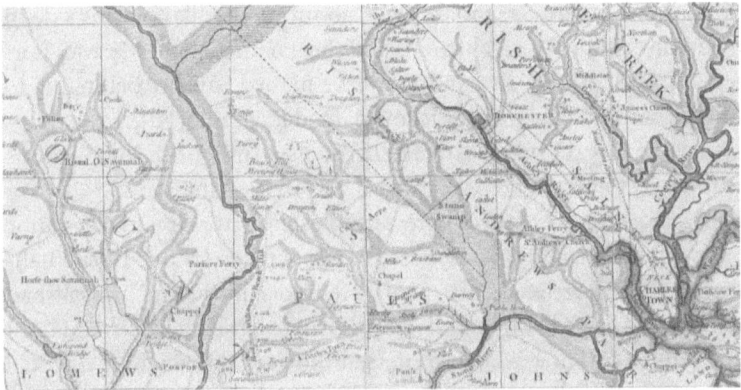

Detail from "A map of South Carolina and a part of Georgia. Containing the whole sea-coast; all the islands, inlets, rivers, creeks, parishes, townships, boroughs, roads, and bridges: As also, several plantations, with their proper boundary-lines, their names, and the names of their proprietors. Composed from surveys taken by the Hon. William Bull Esq. Lieutnant Governor, Captain Gascoign, Hugh Bryan, Esq; and William De Brahm Esqr Surveyor General of the South^n District of North America republished with considerable additions, from the surveys made & collected by John Stuart Esqr His Majesty's Superintendant of Indian Affairs, by William Faden surveyor to the late T. Jeffreys, geographer to the King." Charing Cross [London], 1780. Courtesy of the Library of Congress, Geography and Map Division

Drose of Dorchester, who, with sundry other Negroes as their Captain or chief, went from a Camp of Runaway Slaves at Beach-hill on or about the 22d of June of last Year with Horses, Fire-Arms, Cutlasses and other dangerous Weapons with Intent to, and in the Night did, break open the Dwelling and Stores of the Honorable John Drayton, Esq. at Drayton-Hall and stole and carried away thence Candles, Sugar, Rum, Bacon, Soap, Wine, a Bale of Cloth, and sundry other Articles to a very great Amount, his Property; which Goods Caesar and they carried to the Camp at Beach Hill and divided the Spoil. This Fellow, while the others were taking the Goods, stood centry with a Gun loaded with small-Shot, at the Dwelling House; and in that Case it appeared that if Mr Drayton, or any other Person, had appeared to molest the Thieves, they were to have been shot; providentially this horrid intention was not perpetrated.

There were seven Negroes in and belonging to this Camp, four of whom have been executed at different Times, for the above Fact: One was admitted as evidence; one tried and condemned, but recommended to Mercy by the Magistrates and Freeholders, only, and when interceded with his Honour the Lieutenant Governor without any Hint or Interposition of the Owners, another is yet in the Woods in the Name of Andrew, and is said to be some Times at a

Camp called Back Swamp on Savannah River, about three miles on this side of Mr Galphin's at Silver Bluff.[2] Caesar said that a slave named Sam, Mr. McPherson's property, harbours there; also another Slave named Sancho, belonging to Mr. Liddle of Ponpon, and that another fellow named Isaac alias, N-ger, the property of Mr Stuart of Dorchester, was with them; also Tuffe once Mr Nightingale's, now supposed to belong to Mr Johnson was in the same camp.

Caesar had a ticket to pass any where unmolested with Mr Drose's Name forged to it now in his Custody; Caesar said it was written by one of the half-breed people named Josiah Reed, alias Scott. He also said that he himself had stolen many horses, and that the noted Tilly, a Horse Thief, harboured about the same camp to the Southward. He confessed the Fact for which he suffered and likewise confessed being one of those who robbed and shared the plunder when Mrs Pender was so cruelly beat abused and robbed in April last. He accused two other negroes of being concerned in robbing Mrs Pender, as well as Andrew now out in the woods. All possible Means will be taken to investigate the Truth of his Discovery.

This was one of the most daring Gangs of Fellows that ever infested the Province, and by the spirited Behaviour of the Prosecutor and some other Country Gentlemen offering a handsome Reward withal for the apprehending the said Caesar, he was brought to Justice, being taken up near Silver Bluff and brought from thence to Ashley Ferry. Caesar cost Mr Drase full 520 £ but had he not been so notorious a rogue, yet as the Resolution made in the Commons House of Assembly of this province dated 23rd March 1774 expressly mentions these words "for Felony, Murder, or any other Crime to be hereafter committed" the Magistrates and Freeholders had it not in their Power to do more than give a Certificate for Fifty Pounds Proclamation Money.

1. *South Carolina & American General Gazette,* May 6, 1774.

2. Back Swamp is in the northeast corner of Barnwell County, not far from Augusta, Georgia. Traveling up the Edisto River would have brought the maroons to within about thirty miles of Black Swamp.

During 1775 South Carolina took steps that would eventually lead to full independence from Great Britain. Royal authority quickly collapsed in the face of concerted political opposition, and a new provisional government was created.

Maroons in the Revolutionary and Post-Revolutionary Eras, 1775–1787

CHAPTER THREE

The Revolutionary War in the South was both bloodier and had more of the characteristics of a civil war than in many other locations in North America. On several occasions during the war enslaved people allied themselves with the British in the hope that Governor Dunmore of Virginia's 1775 proclamation—promising freedom to rebel-owned slaves if they joined the British army—would apply throughout the South. In late 1775 Gov. Lord William Campbell, resident on a British ship near Sullivan's Island for his own safety, became something of a magnet for runaway slaves who congregated on the coastal islands north of Charleston, "from whence those villains made mighty sallies, and committed robberies and depredations on the sea-coast of Christ-Church." The South Carolina "company of foot-rangers" eventually attacked the maroons, "burnt the house in which the banditti were often lodged, brought off four negroes, [and] killed three or four." Slaves south of Charleston also took advantage of the confused political situation to flee, and in 1776 the South Carolina Council of Safety was compelled to order that "Capt. Boykin, with 34 Catawba Indians do scout and attempt to take runaway negroes about the Parishes of St George, Dorchester, St Paul and St Bartholomew."[1]

Throughout the course of the Revolutionary War, the sympathies of the enslaved clearly leaned toward the British: slaves with detailed and intimate knowledge of the "back roads" through the swamps surrounding Savannah helped British troops to attack the city in 1778 and guided Loyalist reinforcements from South Carolina away from patriot positions during the siege of Savannah in 1779.[2] About 400 slaves were used to build up the fortifications of Savannah during the siege, but a further 150 were organized into two companies and "armed and equipt as infantry." The Georgia Grand Jury was extremely concerned "that a number of slaves appear in arms and behave with great insolence," but Gov. James Wright believed that the black soldiers had "contributed greatly to our defence and safety" during the joint American and French assault on the city.[3] The lifting of the siege did not mean that these black soldiers were immediately disarmed. In January 1781, long after civilian government had been restored to Georgia, the local Grand Jury complained again about the "number of negroes who are suffered to erect and inhabit houses in and about the town of Savannah and the parish of Christchurch, and who harbour and even protect with fire-arms, negroes runaway from their owners."[4] It is possible that the maroon groups on the Savannah River islands in 1786–87, the subject of most of this chapter, and in particular on Abercorn Island between Ebenezer and Purrysburg, dated from this period. One British force had actually traversed the Savannah River close to where maroons would later take up residence. Perhaps black troops gained firsthand knowledge of these islands while still in the king's service.[5] Black troops continued to serve with the British until the evacuation of Savannah (July) and Charleston (December) in 1782, with upward of a hundred mounted "Black Dragoons" launching disruptive raiding expeditions against patriot forces even while peace negotiations were ongoing in Paris.[6] More than 250 black troops were among the thousands that left with the British as they "had made themselves so obnoxious to their former owners, that dreading the severest punishment, they prayed for protection, and to be permitted to follow the Army," but at least some "were returned to their masters" in accordance with an agreement reached between patriot and Loyalist commanders.[7] Given the chaotic situation in the lowcountry after the departure of the British, with tens of thousands of displaced slaves and numerous disputes over ownership, it is not surprising that rather than return to slavery, some former soldiers chose to take advantage of the situation and make their homes in the Savannah River swamps.[8]

There is additional circumstantial evidence about how maroon groups evolved during the Revolutionary War era. It is clear from advertisements for fugitive slaves placed in the *Royal Georgia Gazette* between 1779 and 1782 that runaways during the American Revolution were significantly different from their predecessors. Nearly 85 percent of colonial runaways were male, and about two-thirds had fled alone. By contrast, more than a third of Revolutionary War runaways were women and children, and more than half fled in groups rather than alone. About a quarter of these ads sought slaves who had fled in family groups consisting of husbands, wives, and young children. It seems probable that these fugitives had decided that the possibility of creating a new life outside of slavery was far more realistic during the chaos of the Revolution and that they were therefore more prepared to take a chance with their entire families. Some fugitive slaves had clear military connections. John G. Williamson sought two slaves in June 1781: "Hercules, a black fellow, about 22 years old, wears a soldier's uniform, red and buff. Jacob, about 19 years old, wears a Hessian uniform." These were just the sort of individuals who might have fought during the siege of Savannah and later tried to keep their newfound independence.[9]

Despite the turmoil of the Revolution, there were no reports of large maroon bands resident in the woods or swamps of South Carolina in the years immediately following the departure of the British. Plantation slavery was gradually reestablished, greatly helped by new importations of slaves direct from Africa.[10] However, in the spring of 1786, just when slaveholders in South Carolina might have started to take the peace and security of their state for granted, Charleston newspapers began to print a series of articles detailing the atrocities committed by maroons on the British Caribbean islands of Dominica and the Bahamas.[11] Within a few weeks two fresh newspaper reports reminded South Carolinians that maroon activity existed in their own backyard. Although the first report in document 3.1 is not categoric, it certainly seems likely that Joseph Williams was killed by maroons in Christ Church Parish, just north of Charleston. The second report, on maroon activity in the northern part of Charleston District close to where the Santee Canal would later be built, makes a clear reference to the killing of Joseph Williams.

1. Journal of the Second Council of Safety, in *Collections of the South Carolina Historical Society* (Charleston: South Carolina Historical Society, 1859), 3:102, 263–64.

2. Benjamin Quarles, *The Negro in the American Revolution* (Chapel Hill: University of North Carolina Press, 1961), 144–45.

3. Frey, *Water from the Rock*, 97–98. Frey's book remains the best account of the black experience during the Revolutionary War. See also Robert Olwell, *Masters, Slaves and Subjects: The Culture of the Power in the South Carolina Lowcountry, 1740–1790* (Ithaca, N.Y.: Cornell University Press, 1998), 243–81; and Minutes of the Governor in Council, October 25, 1779, in Allen D. Candler, "The Colonial Records of the State of Georgia," unpublished typescript, Georgia Archives, 38:2, 230.

4. *Royal Georgia Gazette*, January 18, 1781.

5. Betty Ford Renfro, *River to River: The History of Effingham County, Georgia* (Saline, Mich.: McMaughton-Gunn, 2005), 10.

6. On the "Black Dragoons," see Thomas Bee to Gov. John Matthews, Goose Creek, December 9, 1782, in Thomas Bee Papers, South Caroliniana Library, University of South Carolina, Columbia; and Olwell, *Masters, Slaves, and Subjects*, 258–60.

7. George F. Tyson, "The Carolina Black Corps: Legacy of Revolution (1782–1798)," *Revista/Review Interamericana* 5 (Winter 1975–76): 650–51.

8. Frey, *Water from the Rock*, 211.

9. *Royal Georgia Gazette*, June 28, 1781. See also ibid., October 20, 1780. Statistics relating to runaways have been taken from the extant issues of the *Georgia Gazette* (1763–70, 1774–76) and the *Royal Georgia Gazette* (1779–82).

10. A total of 6,562 Africans were imported into South Carolina in 1783–84. See Frey, *Water from the Rock*, 213.

11. See, for instance, *Charleston Evening Gazette*, January 26, 1786; and *Charleston Morning Post*, February 18, 1786, and April 19, 1786.

3.1] *Maroon activity close to Charleston, 1786*

Charleston, May 18.

On the 9th instant Mr. Joseph Williams of Christ church parish, accompanied by a Mr. Obadiah Baldway, came upon a camp of runaway Negroes, in that parish: They caught two of the Negroes, and were on their return home when they were met in the road by Mr. Charles Gaillard, to whom they related what they had done; which was scarcely concluded when Williams was shot dead by some person, supposed one of the gang at whose camp he had been, and who lay in ambush near the road. This happened about the setting of the sun; the murderer not being pursued got off undiscovered.[1]

So much neglected is that necessary duty of patrolling in the country, that a gentleman has just received a letter from his friend in St. John's parish, Berkeley county, telling him, that gangs of runaway negroes infest the parish, and are doing every species of mischief. So much evil is further apprehended, that it were to be wished Government would send express orders for the officers commanding regiments, to order out detachments against these people, to bring them to a sense of their duty, before some alarming mischief (similar to that in Christ Church Parish) awake their feelings.

We are very well informed, that twenty-two stout black fellows, some with arms, are encamped in the neighbourhood of Watboo,[2] and only a few overseers, poor men, can be procured to go against them.[3]

1. *Columbian Herald or the Independent Courier of North America,* May 18, 1786. The lieutenant governor of South Carolina offered a fifty-pound reward for the capture of the killer(s) (ibid., May 25, 1786).
2. A plantation on the main road north from Moncks Corner adjacent to the western fork of the Cooper River that peters out into marshlands. The Santee Canal, finished in 1800, would cut right through this region.
3. *Charleston Morning Post,* June 15, 1786.

The largest and best-organized maroon group in South Carolina history existed in the Savannah River in 1787, close to where the maroons of 1765 and 1771–72 had been located.

We can never know whether the Savannah River maroons of 1787 were the same individuals who had been causing problems since 1765. They were certainly resident in the same general geographic area, and it is possible that after each group was dispersed by whites it gradually reformed in a suitable alternative location nearby. It is equally possible, however, that captured and killed maroons were replaced by new fugitives who created a successor community from scratch, just coincidentally in the same place. An impenetrable swamp refuge did not cease being an attractive location for fugitives simply because whites periodically managed to organize themselves

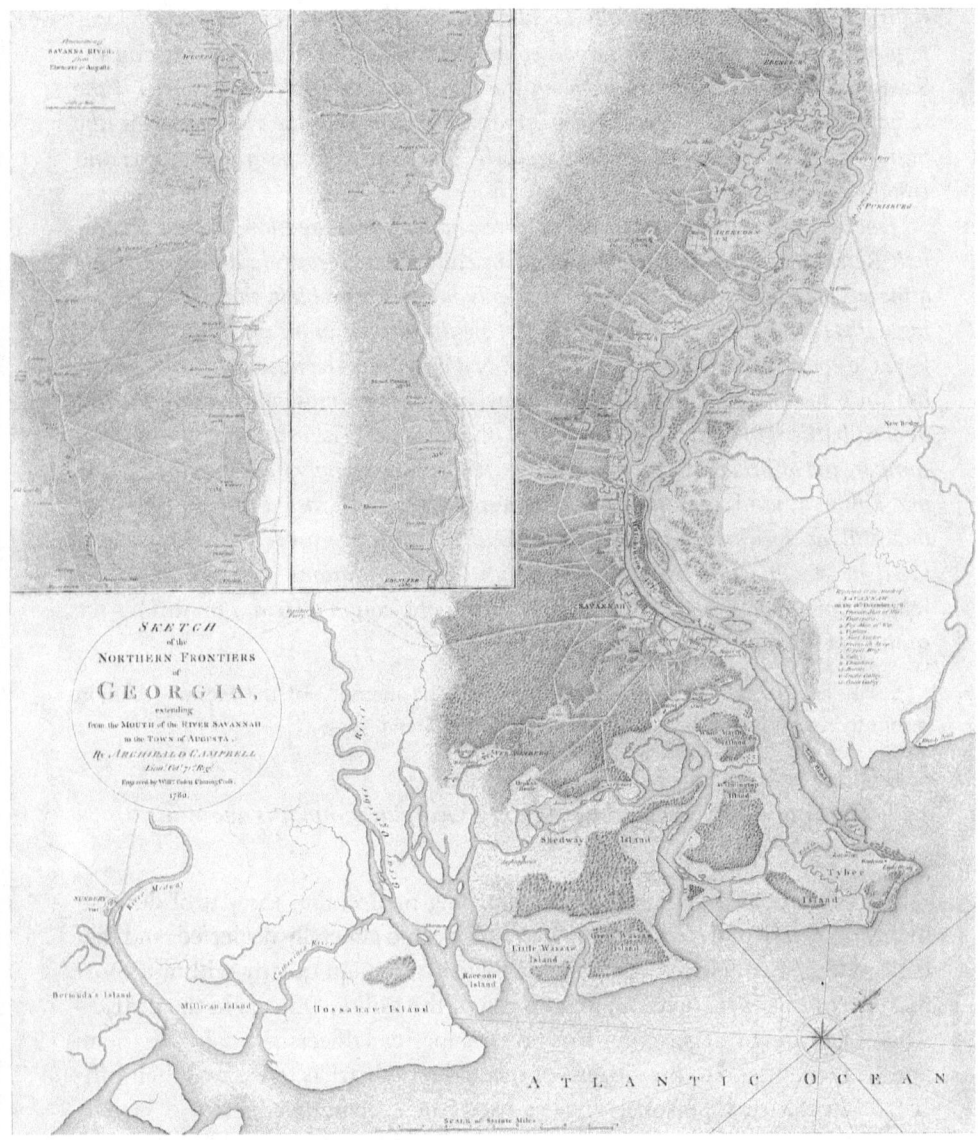

Archibald Campbell, *Sketch of the Northern Frontiers of Georgia.* London: Wm. Faden, 1780.
Courtesy of the Library of Congress, Geography and Map Division

sufficiently to attack it successfully. Local slaves could have learned of the rough location of previously successful maroon communities from enslaved boatmen on the Savannah River who had traded with the maroons, and in this sense, even if the same group was not in continual occupation of camps in the river swamps, the maroons of 1765 could well have figuratively "given birth" to the groups of 1771 and 1786 by their example.[1]

Document 3.2 confirms that the maroons had been on the islands in the Savannah River since at least 1782, but it is unclear how the group had escaped being attacked before 1786 and why they suddenly became a problem that needed dealing with. Documents 3.3, 3.4, and 3.5 cast significant doubt on the ability of white forces to confront the maroons effectively. Not only were the maroons hard to find, but once located they often melted away into the swamps and rarely risked a pitched battle with better-equipped state militia forces. The attacks on the maroon camp by the militia on October 11 and 13, 1786, succeeded only in destroying a camp and killing a handful of maroons. The rest of the group crossed into South Carolina and, as documents 3.4 and 3.5 make clear, for the ensuing four months survived by stealing food and other supplies from plantations. In response to the reports from Gen. James Jackson, the governor of Georgia offered a reward for the capture of the maroons (document 3.6).

1. For an example of this folk memory, see the memory of the Stono Rebellion recounted by a former slave in the 1930s in Smith, *Stono*, 55–56.

3.2] The Grand Jury of Chatham County, Georgia, complains about the activities of runaway slaves[1]

We present, as a grievance of an alarming nature, that the patrol duty, so highly necessary to the well-being of the state is too generally neglected, and that large gangs of runaway Negroes are allowed to remain quietly within a short distance of this town, without an attempt of the Militia Officers in the districts where they are, or of an order from their superior Officers to subjugate them; and we recommend to the citizens of the different districts to elect, as their officers of Militia, such persons as have a fixed residence in this district.

1. Chatham County Superior Court minutes, Grand Jury, October term, 1786, printed in the *Gazette of the State of Georgia*, October 19, 1786.

3.3] Newspapers report on the first engagement between the militia and the Savannah River maroons[1]

A number of runaway Negroes (supposed upwards of 100) having sheltered themselves on Belleisle Island,[2] about 17 or 18 miles up Savannah River, and for some time past committed robberies on the neighbouring planters, it was found necessary to attempt to dislodge them. On Wednesday the 11th inst. a small party of militia landed and attacked them, and killed three or four, but were at last obliged to retreat for want of ammunition, having four of their number wounded. Same evening, about sunset, 15 of the Savannah light infantry and three or four others drove in one of their out-guards, but the Negroes came down in such numbers that it was judged advisable to retire to their boats, from which the Negroes attempted to cut them off, but were prevented by Lieutenant Elfe of the artillery, who commanded a boat with 11 of the company, and had a field piece on board, which he discharged three times with grape shot, and it is thought either killed or wounded some of them, as a great deal of blood was afterwards seen about the place to which the shot was directed. On Friday morning General Jackson[3] with a party proceeded to their camp, which they had quitted precipitately on his approach. He remained till Saturday afternoon, when he left the island, having destroyed as much rough rice as would have made 25 barrels or more if beat out, and brought off about 60 bushels of corn, and 14 or 15 boats and canoes from the landing. He also burnt a number of their houses and huts, and destroyed about four acres of green rice. The loss of their provisions, it is expected, will occasion them to disperse about the country, and, it is hoped, will be the means of most of them being soon taken up.

1. *Gazette of the State of Georgia,* October 19, 1786, reprinted in *Charleston Morning Post,* October 26, 1786, and numerous other newspapers, including the *Georgia State Gazette,* October 28, 1786; *Columbian Herald,* October 30, 1786; and *New York Independent Journal,* November 8, 1786.

2. Now known as Abercorn Island.

3. James Jackson (1757–1806) played a key part in the American Revolutionary War in Georgia and went on to serve in the Georgia legislature and the U.S. Congress. He was governor of Georgia between 1798 and 1801.

3.4] *Gen. James Jackson reports to the governor of South Carolina, Thomas Pinckney, on the engagement with the Savannah River maroons, December 2, 1786*[1]

Sir,

I do myself the honor of addressing you on a subject appearing in my view, of considerable importance to both states. Your Excellency may have heard of the daring banditti of slaves, who some weeks since, attacked two of my detachments, & were at last with difficulty dislodged from their camp on an island in Savannah River. They are now removed to or nigh Hartstones swamp in your state, from whence they frequently make irruptions unto Georgia. About four nights since,[2] upwards of twenty of them armed, attacked the house of Mr

Wolmar, with an intention of taking his life & robbed him of every valuable he possessed. Fortunately for himself he was not at home. Their attacks are not confined to Georgia, every plantation in the Carolina side, has suffered from their depredations. A Mr Guerard[3] in particular, from whence[4] they carry off whole stacks of rice at a time to compensate, as they term it, for their incredible magazine of provisions we destroyed at their camp. The freebooty they reap,[5] and the independent [state][6] they are in, have strong charms of allurement, of course, their numbers are daily[7] increasing. The majority of the runaways are Carolina property, but for the want of officers on your side, they seem to range at large. Nigh[8] one hundred of them armed having been[9] seen a few days since, between Purisburgh & the Union[10]—In short should no immediate step be taken to put a stop to their marauding, as well as well [sic] as to make some severe examples, there is no knowing how far the revolt may lead, or the consequences tend. Should your Excellency, form any plans of co-operation, I shall be ready to meet any officer of yours to concert necessaries meanes, or should you, which I should[11] prefer, make them known to our executive, I shall receive them through that channel.[12]

    1. Joseph Vallence Bevan Papers, Georgia Historical Society, folder 10, item 86. There is a slightly different copy in the Telamon Cuyler Collection, Hargrett Library, University of Georgia, box 82, folder 1: "Slave Rebellion 1786."

    2. November 29, 1786.

    3. Jacob Guerard (d. 1823) owned 5,275 acres in St. Luke's Parish in 1798 and bequeathed property on the Savannah Back River in his will in 1820. He served as a representative for St. Helena's Parish in 1789 and owned 121 slaves in 1790. His brother, Benjamin, was governor of South Carolina from 1783 to 1785. See *Biographical Directory of the South Carolina House of Representatives*, vol. 3: 1775–90 (Columbia: University of South Carolina Press, 1981), 293–94.

    4. In the Telamon Cuyler Collection copy, this is "whose plantation."

    5. In the Telamon Cuyler Collection copy, this is "make."

    6. In the Telamon Cuyler Collection copy, "state" is inserted.

    7. In the Telamon Cuyler Collection copy, this word is omitted.

    8. In the Telamon Cuyler Collection copy, this is "near."

    9. In the Telamon Cuyler Collection copy, this word is omitted.

    10. This could refer either to Union Creek south of Purrysburg or the Union causeway nearer to Savannah.

    11. In the Telamon Cuyler Collection copy, this word is omitted.

    12. In the copy in the Telamon Cuyler Collection, the letter ends with "I have the honor to be your excellency's humble servant. James Jackson B. Genl State of Georgia." This copy of the letter is dated "Savannah December 2d 1786."

3.5] *Gen. James Jackson informs Georgia governor George Matthews of the encounter with the Savannah River maroons*[1]

Sir,

I do myself the honor to inform you of the state this country is again in from the formidable numbers, of runaway slaves, belonging to this, and to the South Carolina state. After we dislodged them from this side, they collected some weeks after in South Carolina, from whence they are in fact much more troublesome to the citizens than when we routed them. Having lost their amazing magazine of provisions, they had in possession, at the time we took their camp. They are compelled to maraud, for their daily subsistence. Twenty of them about four nights since crossed over with an intention of taking the life of Mr Wolmar, whose Negroe, one of their leaders was killed, & whose head was fixed on the western road, in revenge for his life. Fortunately he was not at home, but every valuable he possessed was taken off. Your honor will find by the copy of my letter which I thought myself excusable, considering the exigency, in sending his Excellency the Governor of South Carolina their marauding is not confined to Georgia. Should in consequence of that letter any plans of cooperation, be received by the executive, I flatter myself I shall be honored with them & they shall be as instantly executed. I have before mentioned my fears, & again repeat them. If something cannot be shortly done, I dread the consequences—they are as daring as any & from their independent state, from the ease they enjoy in S. Carolina, forbode what I dread to express, a capital insurrection. Their leaders are the very fellows that fought, & maintained their ground against the brave lancers at the siege of Savannah, & they still call themselves the King of England's soldiers. Let me once more recommend to the executive, through your honor, the fixing a magazine, & the lodging a small sum in the hands of some agent, for contingent expense in this town.

1. Joseph Vallence Bevan Papers, Georgia Historical Society, folder 10, item 87.

3.6] *Georgia governor Edward Telfair offers a reward for each runaway slave caught or killed*[1]

By the Honorable Edward Telfair, esquire,
Captain General Governor and Commander in chief in and over Georgia.
A Proclamation

Whereas good and sufficient information hath been received that a certain Banditti of runaway negroe men who have been out-layers before and since the Evacuation of the Town of Savannah, have lately embodied themselves and have with arms opposed the Militia that have been ordered out to suppress them, and have also committed sundry depredations on the properties of the Inhabitants of the counties of Chatham and Effingham. I have therefore by and with the advice and consent of the Honourable the executive council, thought fit to issue this my proclamation hereby offering a reward of ten pounds for each or either of the said runaway negro men being brought to tryal on good and sufficient proof before a Magistrate of each or either of the said Runaway negro men being killed.

Given under my hand and the Great Seal of the said State at Augusta this twenty-first day of December in the Year of our Lord one thousand and seven hundred and eighty-six, and of our sovereignty and Independence the eleventh.

Edwd Telfair
By his Honors Command
J. Milton Secy
God Save the State.

1. Proclamation Book AAA, 1782–1823, 10–11, Georgia Archives; published in the *Gazette of the State of Georgia*, January 4, 1787.

Documents 3.7 to 3.15 show how information about maroon activity traveled through the official channels of government in South Carolina and how the best course of action was decided upon. Documents 3.11 and 3.12 tell us that once again the Catawba Indians were employed as professional slave hunters, under the supervision of a white commander, but there was also a more coordinated approach between the governments of South Carolina and Georgia.

3.7] *The planter John Lewis Bourquin Jr. writes to his representative in the South Carolina legislature, Joachim Hartstone, on the problems posed by the maroon community, March 14, 1787*[1]

Dear Sir,

I make no doubt but that you have heard of the many depredations which have already been committed by the runaway Negroes about here before your departure for Charleston, & which I can & do assure you that from their threats, unless from your exertion in the House towards their being extirpated I fear in a very short time the prospect of their obtaining provisions will not be their only object as they have in my hearing threatened the lives of many of the citizens amongst which number I am induced to keep a strict caution towards preserving my own safety, as they since your absence paid a visit in our swamp plantation & after some time they left us, with the loss of one Driver fellow, ten barrels of clean rice & myself slightly wounded in the hip. And I have therefore to request of you to make all the exertion in your power, together with the assistance of the rest of the members of our parish either to have the militia arrayed in order to pursue them or otherwise to have by a Proclamation a reward offered for them. It seems that the militia are willing, I mean to say they are ready but not willing to go after them, but as it will require more than a few days to have them entirely extirpated they say there ought to be provisions ordered to be provided for them by the public. I again request of you & the other members as well as for your own as our safety to delay no time, as perhaps the matter may become of too serious a nature as hereafter to give ourselves further trouble about them and more than quietly submit our families to be surprised by them & probably by our own indoor domestics.

I remain dear sir your most obt hble servant
Signed Jno L Bourquin Junr.

1. *Biographical Directory of the South Carolina House of Representatives,* 3:323; and governors' messages, 1786–88, no. 459, South Carolina Archives. John Lewis Bourguin Jr (175?–99) owned one thousand acres in Beaufort District and served as the representative for St. Peter's Parish from 1789 to 1790. He owned forty-five slaves in 1790. See *Biographical Directory of the South Carolina House of Representatives,* 3:81. Joachim Hartstone owned sixteen hundred acres in St. Peter's Parish, eight hundred of which were in Purrysburg. In 1790 he owned forty-seven slaves. He served as the representative for St. Peter's Parish in 1785–86 and 1789–90.

3.8] *Joachim Hartstone recommends action to Peter Porcher and John Fenwicke in the South Carolina Senate, March 15, 1787*[1]

... respecting the banditti of negroes, which if neglected will most certainly prove productive of many evil consequences—even if we follow the example of the Georgians by a proclamation of so much per head—dead or alive—or some other method that you in your wisdom may think proper.

NB If there is any militia law I beg it may be sent up by the first stage.

1. Governors' messages, 1786–88, no. 459.

3.9] *The South Carolina legislature debates an appropriate course of action*[1]

A Message from His Excellency The Governor by His Secretary in the following words.
Mr Speaker & Gentlemen of the House of Representatives
Gentlemen

The letters herewith laid before you, Convey some intelligence concerning Depredations committed by a party of Armed Negroes in the Southern parts of this State which together with such information on the same Subject as can be given by the Members who represent the District so infested will evince the necessity of Establishing an Effectual Militia and patrol Law or of adopting such other measures as you may think the Occasion requires.

Permit me at the same time to draw your attention to the Exhausted State of the Powder Magazines which do not contain a Sufficient quantity of Ammunition for the usual expenditure of the year, and should any extraordinary Occasion require a larger Supply we shall be totally unprovided unless the Legislature devise means of procuring it before they adjourn.

Thomas Pinckney

Charleston 19th March 1787

Ordered That the Message be referred to a Committee, the following Gentlemen were accordingly appointed, Mr. Justice Heyward, General Bull, Mr. Barnwell, Mr. Manner, Mr. Read, Mr. Chisholm, Mr. Fenwicke.

Ordered That a Message be prepared and sent to the Senate, requesting that they would appoint a Committee to Join a Committee of this House on his Excellency's message and the letters accompanying the Message, and that Mr Speaker do sign the same, the following Message was accordingly prepared Vizt.

In the House of Representatives March 19th 1787
Honorable Gentlemen

This House have appointed a Committee on his Excellency's the Governor's Message of this day with two letters accompanying the same Concerning intelligence Concerning Depredations committed by a party of Armed Negroes in the Southern parts of this State.

And this House request that your House will appoint a Committee to join the Committee of this House in order to take the said Message and Letters into Consideration and to Report Speedily thereon. Our Committee are Mr. Justice Heyward, General Bull, Mr. Barnwell, Mr. Manner, Mr. Read, Mr. Chisholm, Mr. Fenwicke.

By order of the House, John Julius Pringle, Speaker

Ordered That the Message be sent to the Senate and that Mr. Barnwell and Mr. John Edward Junr. do carry the same.

A Message from the Senate by their Clerk in the following words Vizt.

In the Senate March 19th 1787
Mr. Speaker & Gentlemen

In answer to your Message Just received, this House inform your House that this House have appointed a Committee to meet the Committee from your House to take into Consideration His Excellency's The Governor's Message of this day, with two letters accompanying the same Conveying intelligence Concerning Depredations committed by a party of Armed Negroes in the Southern parts of this State. Our Committee are General Barnwell, Mr. Middleton & Mr. Garner.

By order of the Senate, John Lloyd, President.

. . .

Mr. Justice Heyward reported from the Joint Committee of both Houses to whom was referred the Message of His Excellency the Governor with two letters accompanying the same, relative to the Depredations committed in the Southern parts of this State by a party of Armed Negroes, which he read in his place and afterwards delivered it in at the Clerks Table where it was again read for information.

Ordered that it be taken into Consideration to Morrow.

And then the House Adjourned 'till to Morrow Morning 9 OClock.

Tuesday March 20th 1787

Read the Journals of Yesterday's proceedings.

The House took into consideration the report from the Joint Committee of both Houses to whom was referred the Message of His Excellency the Governor of this day's date relative to the Depredations committed in the Southern parts of this State by a party of Armed Negroes, with the letters accompanying the same which being read through, was agreed to and is as follows Vizt.

Report That His Excellency The Governor be requested immediately to adopt the most decisive and effectual measures to extirpate the Runaway Negroes committing Depredations in the Southern parts of this State.

That His Excellency be authorized to issue a proclamation offering a reward of Ten Pounds Sterling for each of said Negroes killed or taken in this State.

And that the Legislature will provide for any expence that may be incurred in the prosecution of this business.

Resolved That this house do agree with the Report.

Ordered That the Report and Resolution be sent to the Senate for their concurrence, and that Mr. Thomas Jones and Captain Baker to carry the same.

1. Michael E. Stevens, ed., *Journals of the House of Representatives 1787–1788* (Columbia: University of South Carolina Press, 1981), 236–41. An almost verbatim copy is in the Senate journal, January 1, 1787–March 28, 1787, 229–36, South Carolina Archives. A copy of the original message is in the governors' messages, roll 2, 1786–88, item 459, South Carolina Archives.

3.10] *The South Carolina Privy Council debates action against the maroon community on the Savannah River*[1]

His Excellency laid before the Board the following report from the Senate and House of Representatives, viz.,

In the House of Representatives, March 20, 1787

The joint committee of both houses to whom was referred the letter from the Excellency the Governor, of this day's date, relative to the depredations committed in the southern parts of this State by a party of armed Negroes, with the letters accompanying the same, report

That his Excellency the Governor be requested immediately to adopt the most decisive and effectual measures to extirpate the runaway Negroes committing depredations in the Southern parts of this state.

That his Excellency be authorized to issue a Proclamation offering a reward of ten pounds sterling for cash of said negroes killed or taken in this state.

And that the legislature will provide for any expense that may be incurred in the prosecution of this business.

Resolved, That this house do agree with the report.

Ordered that the report and resolution be sent to the Senate for their concurrence.

By order of the House
J[ohn] S[andford] D[art],
Clerk of the House of Representatives.
In the Senate, March 21, 1787

Resolved that this House do concur with the House of Representatives in the said report and resolution [and that they] be sent to the House of Representatives.

By order of the Senate,
F[elix] W[arley], Clerk of the Senate
Extract from the Journals of the House of Representatives. J[ohn] S[andford] D[art],
Clerk of the House of Representatives.

Upon which his Excellency requested their advice as to the most effectual and decisive measures to put a stop to such depredations.

After due consideration, unanimously agreed that a body of volunteers be selected immediately under the express orders and command of Col. Hutson. Upon the questions be[ing] put as to the number required, Mr Pringle, Col. Gervais were for 60 men, Mr Huger, Dr Tucker 75, W W[ashington] and Maj. Butler 100. It being lost, the deciding number was left to his Excellency to fix on.

His Excellency then requested their advice as to the time for to engage the said men.

Unanimously agreed that they be kept on service for one month certain 3 month, with usual pay of 1/1d with ration from the day that they be called into service and entitled to the reward offered, agreeable to the Resolution of the Legislature on apprehending said Negroes, to any one person.

1. Adele Stanton Edwards, ed., *Journals of the Privy Council, 1783–1789* (Columbia: University of South Carolina Press, 1971), 186.

3.11] *South Carolina governor Thomas Pinckney writes to Col. Thomas Hutson, stationed near Pocotaligo, with instructions, March 23, 1787*[1]

Sir,

In pursuance of the Resolution of the Legislature requesting me to take the most effectual & decisive measures to extirpate the runaway Negroes who have late committed depredations in the vicinity of Purrysburg, I have adopted a plan which I think will be best calculated to effect this purpose & I am happy to find the State has a Officer of your abilities & Integrity commanding the militia of the district infested by these Banditti, to whom with peculiar propriety the execution of this Plan may be intrusted.

As at this Season of the year it would be very inconvenient to keep Militia in the field for a length of time sufficient to suppress this Insurrection, I think a select Body of Men would more effectually answer the purpose & perhaps in the end be less expensive to the State. You will therefore, Sir, be pleased to endeavour to engage a Company of Minute Men in number not exceeding one hundred to serve for one month certain to the pay of one shilling sterling a day, to commence from the time they shall take the field, together with ammunition & Rations will be allowed, this added to the sum of ten pounds sterling for each Negro taken or killed will I hope be encouragement sufficient to procure the number of Men which will be necessary.

The want of accurate information concerning the force & situation of the Negros render it impracticable for me to ascertain precisely the number of men it may be necessary to employ, I must therefore Sir, rely on your discretion, that at the same time you engage a sufficient number to answer the purpose, no unnecessary expense will be incurred.

The appointment of the Captain & Subalterns to command the minute men is also committed to your charge: you will likewise Sir, if you should find it necessary, order out detachments of the Militia to protect the inhabitants until the minute men can be raised if any imergency should require it.

I am in hopes of being able to procure for this service fifteen or twenty Catawba Indians who I apprehend will be particularly useful. They will be directed explicitly to follow your orders & I think should be suffered as little as possible to act alone, as the rewards offered by the Proclamation (copies of which are herewith sent) may be a temptation to abuse. I doubt not you will be particularly careful to prevent any wanton destruction of property, or unnecessary effusion of human blood which you will be better able to do as the certificates to obtain the reward are to come from you.

I have ordered 150 weight of musket powder & 700 weight of lead & 300 flints to be addressed to you by Captain Alexander Davidson who will sail tomorrow for Pocotaligo: with respect to provisions I hope in a very few days to furnish you with money to enable you to purchase for cash, which will be by far the most oeconomincal mode of supplying the Troops, in the meantime you must endeavour to procure what is necessary upon the best terms you can for credit

I am &c

Thos Pinckney.

1. Thomas Hutson (1750–89) owned Cedar Grove plantation in Prince William's Parish and served as representative for that parish in 1779–80, 1782, and 1783–84. See *Biographical Directory of the South Carolina House of Representatives*, 3:366–67; and Thomas Pinckney letterbook, 1787–89, South Carolina Archives.

3.12] *South Carolina governor Thomas Pinckney writes to Colonel Patton at Mr. Harper's, King Street, with instructions to recruit Catawba Indians for use against the maroons, March 26, 1787*[1]

Sir,

In pursuance of the Resolution of the Legislature requesting me to take the most effectual & decisive measures to extirpate the runaway Negros who have late committed depredations in the southern parts of this State, I have determined to engage some Indians to assist in effecting this purpose & as your Residence in the Neighbourhood of the Catawba Indians & the influence you deservedly have among them, will enable you readily to procure their assistance, I have thought proper to entrust you with the power of engaging any number of them not exceeding twenty to serve for a month certain on this Expedition.

You are likewise authorized to employ a citizen of this State to act as their Captain to whom the pay of one dollar a day will be allowed. The Indians shall receive two Blankets each for their Service & will likewise be entitled to receive Ten pounds Sterling for each of the above mentioned runaway Negros whom they shall take, or if they cannot apprehend them, the same reward for each of them whom they shall kill in opposition or endeavour to escape. You will be pleased to inform them that they are to act under the directions of the Commanding Officer of the Militia with whom they are to co-operate. Your drafts for their necessary expenses on their way down shall be punctually discharged.

Give me leave, Sir, particularly to recommend expedition in this business as much of the benefit to the State & the property of the Persons employed will depend thereon.

Thos Pinckney

1. Thomas Pinckney letterbook, 1787–89, South Carolina Archives. Col. Robert Patton (1737–1807) was the representative for various upcountry areas during the 1770s and 1780s, including the Wateree and Catawba rivers.

3.13] *Thomas Pinckney offers a reward for any runaway slave killed or captured*[1]

State of South-Carolina
By His EXCELLENCY
Thomas Pinckney, Esq;
Governor and Commander in Chief in and over the State aforesaid.
A Proclamation.

Whereas a number of fugitive slaves have armed and embodied themselves in the swamps contiguous to Savannah river, and committed divers outrages and depredations on the persons and properties of the good citizens of this state, residing in the vicinity of Purrysburgh, in the parish of St Peter: AND WHEREAS the Legislature, by their Resolution of the twenty-first day of this present month of March, have authorized me to give a reward of *Ten Pounds* sterling for each of the said negroes killed or taken in this state: I DO THEREFORE, by the authority in me vested, issue this my PROCLAMATION, offering a REWARD of TEN POUNDS sterling for every such fugitive slave as shall be apprehended and delivered to the colonel or commanding officer of the militia of the district wherein he shall have been taken, or the sheriff or keeper of the district goal. And in case such fugitive slave or slaves shall oppose or attempt to escape from the person or persons endeavouring to apprehend him or them, so that it may be necessary to kill such slave or slaves, a reward of TEN POUNDS sterling shall be given for every slave killed in such opposition or attempt to escape; a certificate from the said Colonel or Commanding Officer being produced to me by the person claiming such reward, setting forth that he is entitled to the same.

Given under my hand and the great seal of the State in the city of Charleston, this 23d day of March, in the year of our Lord one thousand seven hundred and eighty-seven, and of the sovereignty and independence of the United States of America the eleventh.

Thomas Pinckney.
By his Excellency's command,
PETER FRENEAU, Sec'ry.
God save the State.

1. *State Gazette of South Carolina,* March 26, 1787.

3.14] *Thomas Pinckney writes to Georgia governor George Matthews regarding possible joint operations against the maroon community on the Savannah River, April 2, 1787*[1]

Sir,

The legislature of this state, having requested me to take the most effectual measures to extirpate a number of fugitive slaves, who have armed & embodied themselves in the swamp bordering on the lower parts of Savannah River, & committed depredations on the Inhabitants of the Vicinity. I have directed Col^l Thos Hutson, who commands the militia of the District infested by this Banditti, & to whom the execution of this measure for their Suppression is intrusted, to endeavour to Co-operate with the Commanding Officer of the Forces of the State of Georgia, who may be employed in a similar service. As the Citizens of both States are interested in the reduction of these people, I have no doubt your honor will see the expediency of a joint exertion, & give such directions as you may judge the occasion requires.

I have the honor to be &^ca
Thos Pinckney

1. Thomas Pinckney letterbook, 1787–89, South Carolina Archives. Another copy is in the Joseph Vallence Bevan Papers, Georgia Historical Society, folder 10, item 83.

3.15] *Thomas Pinckney's secretary writes to Col. Thomas Hutson with information on provisions for his troops, April 4, 1787*[1]

Sir,

I am directed by His Excellency the Governor to request you would forward the letter which will be handed to you by Mr John Loveday and directed to the Governor of Georgia, by the first safe opportunity. Mr Loveday will also deliver to you Eighty Pounds Sterling toward the expenses & rations of the Minute Men which are to be raised. In case you have a rec^t for the delivery of one H gal of Rum for the same purpose the General Store Keeper will have orders to send by the same opportunity some powder & ball a particular amount of which will be transmitted to you at the time. The return of Mr Loveday will afford you good opportunity of communicating to the Governor any intelligence you may have received & see occasion to give.

I am sir
S Ruiston
NB Rec^t for the rum signed Jno Anthony 3^d April 1787. 110 Gallons.

1. Thomas Pinckney letterbook, 1787–89, South Carolina Archives.

Documents 3.16 to 3.20 give an immense amount of detail about the battles that took place between the maroons and white militia forces on April 21 and May 6, 1787. The maroons had returned to the Savannah River islands, not far from where their camp had been in October 1786. This camp was even larger than the one that had been destroyed six months previously and had either been rapidly built in the intervening period or, more likely, was a secondary base that had existed before the battles of 1786. If the twenty-one houses mentioned in document 3.18 were of a similar size to plantation dwellings for slaves, then they could have housed up to two hundred people. In addition to being large, the new camp was well defended and well hidden: it took the militia five days of searching to find it.

3.16] *Newspapers report the next encounter between the militia and the maroons on the Savannah River*[1]

The legislature of South Carolina, taking into consideration the daring state of the runaway slaves, ordered, at their last session, a company of minutemen, and a draft of the Granville County Militia, for the purpose of keeping the field 'till they are totally broken up. Col. Hutson commanding them, stationed at Purysburgh, is now waiting for cooperation with this state. Last Saturday evening[2] the Colonel detached Capt. Winkler, with three boats, and about 25 men, to waylay Collin's creek.[3] About eight or nine o'clock one of Capt Winkler's boats discovered four of their canoes, full of men, coming down the creek, when a warm skirmish took place, which ended in favour of the white people. Louis, one of their Majors, formerly belonging to Col. Stirk,[4] and last to Commodore Bowen,[5] was killed, and two others (seen to fall overboard) were supposed to have shared his fate, as the canoe with Louis fell into Capt. Winkler's hands, and the boat waited 15 minutes without any sign of their rising. Had not Capt Winkler detached his other boats, the whole of the negro party must have been killed or taken. Two of the Carolinians were slightly wounded, one in his hand and arm, the other in his face.

1. *Gazette of the State of Georgia*, April 26, 1787, reprinted in the *State Gazette of South Carolina*, May 10, 1787; *Columbian Herald*, May 10, 1787; and *Georgia State Gazette*, May 19, 1787.
2. April 21, 1787.
3. Now known as Big Collis Creek.
4. Col. John Stirk.
5. Oliver Bowen (1741–1800), commodore of the navy, purchased 850 acres on the Great Ogeechee River in 1775 (Colonial Deed Book DD, 1775–98, 17, 26, Georgia Archives). He was a resident of Savannah, according to the 1798 Chatham County tax digest. See *Georgia Genealogical Magazine* 29 (July 1968): 1963.

3.17] *Georgia governor George Matthews writes to Brigadier General Jackson, April 26, 1787*[1]

Sir

I received your favor of the 23^d instant inclosing a letter from Col. Hutson the business of the Negroes the Executive had taken up some days before the receipt of yours. The order taken thereon was forwarded by Mr Baldwin which gives you full power as far as the law supports you as an officer. I, with you, Sincerely regret the defects in the militia law but am well assured you are fully satisfied the Executive cannot remedy the defect. The Council have ordered a draft for thirty pounds in your favor, to inable you to pay the express and purchase ammunition.

1. Governors' letterbooks, 1786–94, Georgia Archives.

3.18] *Military dispatch from Col. James Gunn to Brig. Gen. James Jackson, May 6, 1787*[1]

Sir,

Lieut Col Howell informed me at one o'clock this morning that the negroes were encamped in Bear Creek. At half past ten o'clock I discovered some signs of them in the swamp belonging to the estate of Patton, a few miles below Zubley's ferry,[2] their camp was situated on the lower side of Bear Creek,[3] it was 700 yds in length, & about 120 in width. They had thrown the logs & cane that came out of the cleared ground, into a kind of breech work about 4 feet high, the place they went in & out at, would admit but one person to pass at a time. Their sentry was about 150 yds advance down the creek, about two miles below their camp they had fallen large logs across the creek in order to prevent boats passing up (small canoes might pass at high water) as soon as I discovered their sentry, I ordered Lieut. Lemden with eight men to rush on, fourteen of the light infantry followed with charged bayonets, Capt Tattnall with the remainder of the detachment moved on the right, with as much expedition as the nature of the ground would admit of. Major McPherson with a detatchment of South Carolina militia, & fifteen of the Catawabah Indians composed the second line. As soon as the negroes discovered that the troops had got into their encampment, they run into the swamp firing a few shot at random, they were pursued two miles in every direction the swamp would admit of. They left six of their head men, dead on the ground, the parties that pursued them, found many blankets covered with blood, I have every reason to believe there were many of them wounded. Their baggage & provisions were taken, & the Indians got as many good blankets & clothing of different kind, as they were able to take with them. I ordered Lieut Col. Howell with his detatchment to search the swamp as high as the ferry. At five o'clock I had their houses (21 in number) & the works set on fire. The whole of the cleared land was planted in rice and potatoes. The great fatigue the men had undergone, for four days, made it necessary to retire to some place, where they might be refreshed. Maj. McPherson returned to Purysburgh, & the Chatham detatchment, to Abercorn. I shall return to Savannah with the troops in the morning, as keeping them longer on command in my opinion would be of no advantage to the state, but a great injury to those individuals whose lot it was to be in the first draft, as it chiefly fell on men of small property, the men of large fortune & who were more particularly interested in the destruction of the runaways, being generally defaulters, the depreciation of the paper money reducing the fine to a mere trifle. It is with pleasure that I inform you there was not one white man killed. Lieut Fitzgerald of the light infantry was slightly wounded in the side.

1. Joseph Vallence Bevan Papers, Georgia Historical Society, folder 10, item 84. Col. James Gunn (1753–1801) served as one of Georgia's first two senators in congress.
2. A few miles north of Purrysburg on the north bank of the Savannah River.
3. Bear Creek together with Big Collis Creek form the western boundary of an island in the Savannah River, with the main river channel forming the eastern boundary.

3.19] *Newspapers report the second encounter between the militia and the maroon community on the Savannah River*

A gentleman just arrived from Savannah informs, that a party of 120 men were going against the runaway negroes, who are assembled in great force about twenty miles from Savannah. When the gentleman was on his way he heard the firing of cannon, which probably arose from an engagement.[1]

In consequence of the order of the Executives of the two states a co-operation against the banditti of runaway slaves commenced on the 1st instant, and a junction of the troops under Col. Gunn and Major McPherson, agreeable to a concerted plan, took place at the old camp in the fork of Abercorn and Collin's Creek, leaving Capt Lloyd's Artillery at the commanding pass of each. On the evening of the 5th Lieut Col. Howell, who was likewise ordered to proceed from Ebenezer down Bear Creek, and put himself under the command of Col. Gunn, discovered the negro camp in Patton's swamp, of which he gave notice to that officer. The Colonel advanced, Major McPherson, with the Carolinians and 15 Catawba Indians, forming a second line;—fortunately their centry was killed, when he ordered the advance under Lieut. Lewden to rush on, supported by the Town Light Infantry, who entered a breastwork the negroes had thrown up with charged bayonets. As soon as the negroes saw their work stormed, and the other troops, commanded by Major McPherson and Capt. Tattnall, filing off to their right and left, after a few random shot, they fled on every quarter, leaving six of their head-men dead on the field—only one white man of both detachments, a Serjeant of the Light Infantry, being slightly wounded. Many others of the Negroes are supposed wounded; as several blankets were picked up, in different directions, on scouring the swamp, clotted with blood. Twenty-one houses were destroyed, and seven boats taken.

It is said that the Carolinians and Indians have since killed two more; and by a man who was present we are informed, that Capt. Dasher,[2] with a small party of the Effingham militia, had fallen in with 18 on their way to the Indian nation, killed a man and a boy, taken nine women and children, Major Louis (who was thought to have been killed in Collin's Creek) and six more escaping. Sharper is said to be still in the swamp with several others, and it is supposed was in the party the Carolinians and Indians fell in with.

A correspondent observes, that the late decisive effort made by Col. Gunn to break up the camp, and destroy the confidence and strength of the runaways, cannot fail of producing the best effects, as they had got seated and strongly fortified in the midst of an almost impenetrable swamp, and opening a general asylum, which no doubt would have been embraced by many on the approach of hot weather. Indeed running away had already become more prevalent than usual. When it is recollected how long a band of these people have rebelled, and opposed with success, the government of Jamaica, and look at the still more recent example to the southward of us, in the Dutch government of Surinam, where, from being contemptible fugitives at first, they at length fixed and fortified the recesses, and, (what will always take place where persons of any description are in the practice of independence and threatened with extreme danger) with the increase of numbers, they exercised the principle of union, and opposed and harrassed their masters until they were obliged to treat with them; and they are now an actual independent colony, the example of which is felt as the greatest inconvenience. But what such establishment will finally issue in is not in human foresight to determine. It is, perhaps, the wish of interest, as well as of Philosophy, that they were all in Africa. In this country, it is said, that some of the Negroes who formed the late camp have been in state of rebellion ever since the peace; and that some of them had been employed in arms by the British in the late war. To have despised or neglected them, or permitted their robberies, might have led them on to equally ambitious and extensive views with those of Jamaica or Surinam, where the best stationary regiments could not subdue them. The destruction of the camp, killing their leaders, and dispersing the rest, with their women and children, will, it is hoped, prevent any attempt of the kind again soon. The Colonel, it is said, highly commends the conduct of his officers and men.[3]

1. *Charleston Morning Post,* May 8, 1787.

2. John Martin Dasher (1738–1802) was commissioned as a second lieutenant in the Grenadier Company of lower St. Matthew's Parish in 1776. See Allen D. Candler, ed., *Revolutionary Records of the State of Georgia* (Atlanta: Franklin-Turner, 1908), 1:220.

3. *Gazette of the State of Georgia,* May 10, 1787, reprinted in *Georgia State Gazette,* May 19, 1787, and *Columbian Herald,* May 28, 1787.

3.20] *Newspapers report on the aftermath of the battles between the militia and the maroons*

May 17, 1787

The camp of runaway negroes on Savannah River seems to be now totally broke up, some of them are coming in daily to their owners; and there is no doubt but their leader Sharper has been killed by the Carolinians and Indians.

CAPTURED by Capt. Dasher and part of his company, the following NEGROES, viz. *Fatima* and *Hannah,* who say they belong to John Graham; *Phillis* and boy *Sharper,* say they belong to Mrs. Wright; *Nancy* and *Patience,* who say they belong to Mr. Philip Ulmer; and now in my custody. The owners of the above negroes may have them on proving their property and paying charges; they are desired to apply as early as possible there being no gaol in the county I cannot be accountable for escapes.

Tho[s] Lane, Sheriff

Ebenezer, May 8, 1787.[1]

May 24, 1787

By the vigilance and activity of Israel Bird,[2] Esq, of Canouchie[3] and some of his slaves, Lewis (second in command of the gang of runaway negroes lately routed by Col. Gunn) was taken last week, and brought to town on Saturday. Last Monday he was tried, and being found guilty of robbery &c he was sentenced to be hanged on the 9th June next.[4]

May 31, 1787

Brought to the Workhouse

A NEGRO WENCH, who called herself Juliet, and says she belongs to Godin Guerard, Esq, South Carolina

May 14, 1787

A NEGRO WENCH, who calls herself Peggy, says she belongs to Godin Guerard, Esq,

May 16, 1787

Both these negro wenches say they were amongst the runaway negroes in Abercorn swamp.

Frederick Long[5]

1. *Gazette of the State of Georgia,* May 17, 1787. The child Sharper may well have been the son of the maroon leader of the same name.

2. Israel Bird was a captain in the Effingham County Militia in 1785; see *Gazette of the State of Georgia,* March 24, 1785.

3. The Cannouchee River branches off the Ogeechee River into Bryan County south of Savannah and then forms part of the border between Bryan County and Liberty County.

4. *Gazette of the State of Georgia,* May 24, 1787, reprinted in *Georgia State Gazette,* June 16, 1787, and *Columbian Herald,* June 7, 1787.

5. *Gazette of the State of Georgia,* May 31, 1787. These women testified at Lewis's trial.

The trial record of one of the leaders of the Savannah River maroons (document 3.21) tells us about the familial nature of the settlement and its internal military organization. A significant piece of information in the trial record is that Sharper chose an alias for himself, Captain Cudjoe, that recalled the successful military leader of the Jamaican maroons in the 1730s.[1] It suggests that knowledge of the maroons of Jamaica had penetrated the consciousness of mainland slaves as well as slaveholders, either through the careless talk of owners or, perhaps more likely, directly from slaves imported from the island into Savannah.[2] A Georgia planter remarked in 1775 that "Negroes have a wonderful art of communicating intelligence among themselves; it will run several hundreds of miles in a week or a fortnight."[3]

1. Richard B. Sheriden, "The Maroons of Jamaica, 1730–1830: Livelihood, Demography and Health," in *Out of the House of Bondage,* ed. Heuman, 154.

2. For an example of a cargo of Jamaican slaves arriving in Savannah, see *Gazette of the State of Georgia,* April 12, 1787.

3. Morgan, *Slave Counterpoint,* 476.

3.21] *Trial record of Lewis forwarded to the governor of Georgia by Savannah magistrates*[1]

Savannah 21st May, 1787

Sir,

We take the earliest opportunity to inclose to your Honor, the proceedings, of the court, met this day for the trial of Negro Lewis, who was convicted and sentenced as the minutes point out.

As the sentence cannot be carried into execution, till your Honor's determination be had agreeably to the act of assembly, no time has been lost in making the communication, and we hope sufficient time has been allowed, for your Honor's order in the Business.[2]

We have the honor to be yr very obt servts

Dav^d Montaigut J.P.

W. Stephens

Justus H Scheuber J. P.

At a Meeting of the Justices for the trial of a negroe man Slave named Lewis the property of Oliver Brown esq^r for the Murder of John Casper Herman,[3] Robbing Philip Ulmer,[4] John Lowerman of Georgia and Col^l Bouquin of South Carolina this 21^t May 1787.

Present David Montaigut, William Stephens, Justus H. Scheuber, Benjⁿ L. Lond, Esquires Justices of the peace.

The State vs Lewis a Negroe

Negroe Lewis brought up says he belongs to Oliver Bowen charged as above.

The following Jurors drawn and sworn as the Law directs: William Oakman 1 Thomas Mitchell 2 Stephen Britton 3 Isaac Laroach 4 William Lewden 5 Asa Emanuel 6 Levi Sheftall 7

Evidences Betty [sic][5] and Juliet, negroe women.

Lewis being called on by the Court, proceeded to relate the following narrative. Says his Masters White Overseer used him ill and he ran away and joined Sharper (who belonged to Alexander Wright[6]) and Jemmy who belonged to Philip Ulmer) in Martins Swamp, That Sharper gave Jemmy a gun and told him to fire at White people, which Jimmy did and wanted the prisoner to keep Centry which he refused—On which Sharper told the prisoner to move off which he also refused; that ten negro men were with them and a number of women in their Camp. That Joe belonging to Bourquin gave the prisoner a gun and they all lived together until the White people first came up, That then Sharper and the prisoner disagreed and Separated, Sharper had twenty Soldiers and was called Captain Cudjoe and that he the prisoner was called Capt Lewis, he say's that he was absent near two years says that he called on Mr Thomas Pollhill[7] and told him to take Care of the runaway Negroes, or by'e and by'e, they would Come and hurt him, Say's that the great Coat he has on belongs to Mr Lowerman, That he saved Mr Bourquin and John Walthour from being killed, That himself Lewis, Sharper, and ten other negroes met John Casper Hersman and One other White person in a Boat in the Long reach, Savannah River, with Corn and potatoes; Sharper hailed the boat and after talking with them let the boat pass. Afterwards, Lewis, Cupid & Fortune Met Hersman, in Martins old field going to the negro Camp, Hersman asked the prisoner where Sharper and Lewis were; the prisoner said Master don't you know me my name is Lewis Hersman begged the prisoner to carry him to the Camp which he refused, as he wanted Victuals of which he was in search, That Hersman waited at a fire from sunsett that Evening untill day break next morning then the prisoner took Hershman along to Camp in Company with him after which Sharper said Lewis had no business to bring White people to camp; That Chicheum[8] who belonged to Mr

Guerard (whose head is now at the Spring hill) killed Mr Hersman, immediately at his landing—That he had no Concern in it, that the Murder was committed as above on which he Separated camp with Sharper. That he had a gun in a Canoe in Company with another negroe; That Peter, belonging to Herriat and Dembo, belonging to Guerard fired at Capt Winkler's men that Dembo was killed and the others made their Escape That Sharper is not killed, as he knows of That he was going to his Master's Mills on Ogeeche,[9] with a number of negroes When Capt Dasher fell in with the party, and took several and killed others, That after this he killed a Calf in Ogeeche, and was taken by two negroes belonging to Mr Bird—who took his gun from him—Says all the negroes killed Cattle at Abercorn—The prisoner took Corn at Mr Greenhows.[10] Peter took Sheep from there; the prisoner & Sharper wanted to Chop him for Stealing Mr Greenhow's sheep, he was also present when Cattle was killed in Carolina.

Juliett belonging to Mr Guerard says—that she with her husband Pope now killed run away last Christmas and Went to Sharper and Lewis the prisoner, at their camp (and planted rice) Says that Sharper was head Man, and Lewis Captain for Sharper, all the women Stayed in Camp, Says Lewis she heard met with a White Man and Conducted him to the Camp—That Chicheum by Sharpers Orders killed him and then threw him in to a pond as she was informed, and that Lewis was present. She heard the gun fire in the morning soon—That Sharper and Lewis going to fetch more of Mr Guerards hands was fired on by White people and two negroes were killed on which they returned, That Lewis was in Camp with a gun when the Militia routed them, Sharper ordered all the women in the Canes—Lewis and Sharper frequently Quarrelled though generally together—Sharper was head Man and called Captain Cudjoe Who Commonly Ordered Lewis out though he refused, The Beef was Commonly brought to Camp by Joe; and Lewis killed a Cow one day, Says Lewis was on the party that plundered Lowerman and brought his Cloths to Camp when Lewis had some white Linen &c.

Peggy belonging to Mr Guerard run away with her husband named little Coke and went to Sharper, Says Lewis was in camp and she knows him very well, Sharper was head man, and Lewis next; Lewis went to Ulmers with Frank and plundered him as she heard Lewis and Frank say, That, Sharper and Lewis with the other men in a number of Boats went to Mr Bourquins and Stole rice, Lewis had two Bushels rice—every Body shared rice Lewis with Dembo and Frank where going to Mr Guerards plantation to fetch more negroes, they all had guns, got powder at Lowermans, and at a White Woman's in Carolina, Dembo and Frank were killed, Lewis Conducted Hersman, half way to Camp Sharper said Lewis had no Business to Carry White people to Camp and Sent the Soldiers, all negro men who had guns, Chicheum, little Cook, Frank, Dembo, Joe & Dick), Chicheum killed Hersman and Lewis was present, Sharper quarrelled with Lewis for bringing Hersman to Camp, She heard the gun fire at Breakfast time. That Lewis had a gun when the fight begun with the other negroes, woman all run into the Canes; saw Lewis with White linen and a great Coat which he said he got from Lowerman, Saw beef brought from the Carolina side by Lewis, says she heard Hersman was put in a pond; Chicheum had his Cloths; says Lewis Quarrelled with Sharper, because he did not get his share of plunder, after which Lewis got his part—that Lewis plundered frequently had a gun and Cloths &c.

Juliett—again says Lewis wanted his own people as Sharper took all his men

The Jury brought in the following Verdict. We find the prisoner guilty Levi Sheftall foreman

The justices Sentenced the Negroe Lewis to be hanged on the South Common by the Neck until he shall be Dead on the Ninth day of June next at ten o'clock in the Morning; After Which his head to be Cut of and Stuck upon a pole to be sett up on the Island of Marsh opposite the Glebe land in Savannah River, in which the jury acquiesced, the justices having thought it Advisable to take their opinion thereon.

Clerk's Office, Chatham County.

Extract from the minutes this 21st May 1787.

The Jury and Justices appraised the negro Lewis at thirty pounds Sterling.[11]

---

1. Telamon Cuyler Collection, box 71, folder 12: Georgia Slavery Trials, Hargrett Library, University of Georgia.

2. Sec. 8 of the 1770 Georgia slave code stipulated that all capital sentences must be suspended and referred to the governor until "his pleasure be known thereon" (an act for ordering and governing slaves, in *A Digest of the Laws of the State of Georgia*, ed. Robert Watkins and George Watkins [Philadelphia: R. Aiken, 1800], 167).

3. John Caspar Hirschman appears in the Ebenezer Church Record Book as the father of Elisabeth, baptized May 27, 1775, and Salome, born January 16, 1779. His marriage to Rosina Keubler on January 31, 1764, is also recorded. See George F. Jones and Sheryl Exley, eds., *Ebenezer Record Book, 1754–1781* (Baltimore: Genealogical Publishing, 1991), 69, 78, 91. He might well be the "son of the wealthy Caspar Hirschmann, who came here with the third Swabian transport [1752] along with his two parents, who died some years ago at Halifax in Georgia" mentioned in George Jones, ed., *Detailed Reports on the Salzburger Emigrants* (Athens: University of Georgia Press, 1993), 17:190, entry for June 1760. Halifax was located on the Savannah River fifty miles above Ebenezer. See George Jones, *The Georgia Dutch: From the Rhine and Danube to the Savannah, 1733–1783* (Athens: University of Georgia Press, 1992), 150.

4. Philip Ulmer (d. 1806) owned twenty slaves in 1793 and was listed as a resident of Cherokee Hill plantation in 1798, in the most northerly part of Chatham County bordering Effingham County and the Savannah River (*Georgia Genealogical Magazine* 30 [October 1968]: 2049).

5. This individual is called Peggy later in the document.

6. Son of Sir James Wright, Georgia's last colonial governor.

7. Thomas Polhill served on the Effingham County Grand Jury (*Gazette of the State of Georgia,* March 24, 1785).

8. This is an unusual name and is perhaps evidence of Native American ancestry.

9. The Ogeechee River forms the southern boundary of Chatham County, and Oliver Bowen did own property there; see item 3.16, note 5.

10. James Greenhow owned Hampton plantation near Abercorn. He advertised for several "strayed or stolen" cattle in the *Gazette of the State of Georgia,* December 9, 1784.

11. On the back of this document is written "Order taken 26 instant Pardons," indicating that the case was referred to the pardons committee.

3.22] *Georgia's Executive Council confirms death sentences for rebels*[1]

May 26, 1787.

A letter dated 21st May inst from David Montaigut, William Stephens and Justus H. Scheuber esquires Justices of the Peace for the County of Chatham inclosing the proceeding of the court, met for the trial of Negro Lewis, was received and read.

Whereupon the board approved of the Sentence and Order.

That the Sec^y of the State do prepare a warrant for carrying the degree of the said court in execution against Negro Lewis on the 9th day of June next.

20 June 1787

A letter from William Holzendorf and John Spencer esqrs two of the Justices of the County of Effingham inclosing the proceedings of a Court held in the said County on the 12th inst for the Tryal of a Negro Dick, the property of the Estate of Clem^t Martin Deceased.

Ordered

That the Sentence of the said Court by carryed into execution at the time & place appointed and that the S^y of the State do prepare a Warrant for the Purpose.

1. Georgia Executive Council minutes, 1786–89, Georgia Archives.

3.23] *Newspaper report of Lewis's execution*[1]

Last Saturday Lewis, one of the head-men of the camp of runaway negroes lately broke up, was executed pursuant to his sentence.

1. *Gazette of the State of Georgia,* June 14, 1787.

The aftermath of the destruction of this maroon community saw petitions for compensation from slave owners who had lost slaves during the battles (document 3.25) and invoices being settled (document 3.26). A different perspective comes from the report of the entire affair from an abolitionist standpoint (document 3.24).

3.24] *An abolitionist viewpoint*[1]

Accounts from the southward, assure us, that hostilities of a serious nature, have commenced in Carolina and Georgia, between the citizens of those States, and the runaway negroes, who having fled from their task-masters to the wilderness, have been thither pursued by the forces of those States, attacked and defeated. It is, however, apparent, from these accounts, that those brave and hardy sons of Africa, will occasion those States the loss of much blood and treasure, before they are subjugated—as notwithstanding their sufferings in their present exposed situation—their want of military apparatus to defend themselves—and their late defeat, the appearance of submission is not discoverable among them—Though vanquished they are not disheartened—and they seem wisely to prefer a precarious existence, in freedom, on the barren heath, to the chains of their oppressors, whose avarice, cruelty and barbarism encreases with their wealth—in short the spirit of liberty they inherit appears unconquerable. Heaven grant it may be invincible.

1. *Massachusetts Centinel,* June 23, 1787.

3.25] *Petitions for compensation from the owners of slaves killed in 1787*

Saturday 12 January 1788[1]

On the Petition of John Lourman, praying to be paid for a Negro killed among the Runaway Negroes—Your Committee are of opinion the prayer of the Petition ought not to be granted, which was agreed to.

On petition of Gorden Guerard,[2] praying to be paid for sundry negroes killed in arms against this State.

Your Committee are of opinion the prayer of the Petition ought not to be granted, which was agreed to.

Wednesday the 4th February 1789.[3]

Your committee have also had under consideration the petition of Oliver Bowen Esq[r] setting forth the conviction and execution of a Negro fellow named Lewis belonging to him and praying payment it is the opinion of the committee the prayer of this petition is reasonable and recommend that it be RESOLVED that His Honor the Governor in Council be authorized to draw a Warrant on the Treasury in favor of Oliver Bowen for the sum of forty pounds.[4]

1. Georgia House journal, 1788, 285–87, Georgia Archives.

2. Godin Guerard, brother of Jacob and Benjamin, owned a plantation in Prince William's Parish. In 1785 he advertised for sixteen runaways from his plantation, believing that "it is more than probably they will attempt to conceal themselves on or near Savannah River" (*Gazette of the State of Georgia,* May 12, 1785). The South Carolina legislature did compensate Godin Guerard for "the Negroes hanged at Beaufort," but it is not known if these slaves had been part of the maroon community on the Savannah River. The claim is contemporary to the one he made to the Georgia legislature (South Carolina General Assembly Papers, series S165005, 1788, no. 128, dated February 5, 1788).

3. Georgia House journal, 1789, 152, Georgia Archives.

4. Despite this resolution, there is no mention either in the executive journals of the governor or in the state treasury ledgers from this period that this sum was ever paid to Oliver Bowen. The 1770 slave code made provision for compensation to be paid to owners of executed slaves, though there was no similar provision for owners of slaves killed by the militia. See Watkins and Watkins, *Digest,* 169.

3.26] *Counting the cost of fighting the maroons* [1]

Mr President and Honorable Gentlemen of the Senate
Honorable Gentlemen

Application has lately been made to me for the pay of the Militia who were employed in the service of suppressing the armed fugitive slaves in the southward part of the State. As the Law now in existence for the Regulation of the Militia does not ascertain whether they are to receive pay for similar services & I am informed no farther regulation respecting them has taken place during the present sitting I am constrained thus late in the session to request that the Legislature will determine whether they shall receive any & what pay when called into the field on services of this nature.

An account of expenditures in suppressing the insurrection of the Negroes is herewith transmitted.

Thomas Pinckney

Charleston the 26th February 1788

An account of expenditures attending the dispersing the Fugitive Slaves near Purrysburg for taking & killing such of said Fugitives by the Militia & the Catawba Indians under the command of Lieut Colo Thomas Hutson of the Lower Granville Regiment.

Account of monies paid by Colo Hutson vizt

1787
April   15th   To cash pd Wm Sanders express riding as pr
               Voucher   £1.8..
        17   do pd Wm McFarlane for a pot as per ditto   £ . 9. 4.

	19	d⁰ pᵈ Davᵈ Saussy as per Voucher²	£16..	
	21	d⁰ pᵈ Jno Morgindollar Waggon hire as pʳ d⁰	£2.2..	
May	3d	d⁰ pᵈ Davd Saussy as per d⁰	£30..	
	4	d⁰ pᵈ D⁰ balance in full as pʳ a/c recᵗˢ	£47.4.4	
October	25ᵗʰ	d⁰ pᵈ in the Treasury Cash in hand	£32.16.4	£130.0..
		To cash pᵈ by order of His Excellency the Governor vizᵗ		
		For 1 HHead of Rum	110 Gall	
		@ 2/8 & dray hire	£14.14.4	
		To Jno Loveday carrying Dispatches &ᶜᵃ to Col⁰ Huston	£2.10.0	
		To cash pᵈ into the Treasury	£2.15.8	£20...
		To cash pᵈ by Order of His Honor the Lieut Govʳ Vizᵗ		
May	18ᵗʰ	Captᵗ Thoˢ Patton for scalps taken by the Catawba Indians under his command	£40.0..	
		d⁰ d⁰ provisions for the Indians	£.18.10	
		d⁰ d⁰ for his pay as Capt of ditto	£6.15.4	
June	9ᵗʰ	To cash pᵈ Jno Lloyd junʳ for blankets for ditto	£20.7.6	£68.1.8
August	14ᵗʰ	To Jacob Winkler for killing one of the Fugitives (Govʳˢ Order)	£10...	
Septʳ	20	Nath Zettler for d⁰ d⁰ d⁰ (per d⁰ d⁰)	£10...	
Decʳ	5	Doctor's bill for attending & dressing one of the wounded	£3...	£23..
				£241.1.8

February 28ᵗʰ, 1788³

The House took into Consideration the Report of the Committee to whom was referred his Excellency the Governors message of the 26ᵗʰ instant relative to an Application lately made to his Excellency for the pay of the Militia who were employed in the Service of Suppressing the armed fugitive Slaves in the Southern part of this State, which being read through

Resolved That the Militia who were employed in the Service of Suppressing the armed Fugitive Slaves in the Southern parts of this State as mentioned in the Governors message of the 26ᵗʰ instant by reason of the Resolves of the Legislature of the 20ᵗʰ March 1787 on the Subject and the extraordinary Circumstances of the said Militia so employed being carried out of this State into the State of Georgia, and being embodied for the time requisite for the Suppression of said Negroes be intitled to receive the following pay Vizt.

Field Officers, Seven Shillings per day
Captains, Five Shillings per day
Subalterns, Three Shillings & Six pence per day

Non Commissioned Officers, One Shilling & Six Pence per day
Privates, One Shilling per day

Ordered that the Resolution be sent to the Senate for their Concurrence and that Doctor Lynah and Mr. Smelie do carry the same.

1. Governor's messages, 1788, no. 459, South Carolina Archives.
2. Saussy's enclosed voucher was for "purchasing rice & beef for the benefit of a detachment of the Lower Granville County Reg.t Militia."
3. Stevens, ed., *Journals of the House of Representatives 1787–1788*, 525. This was agreed by the Senate the following day.

South Carolina governor Thomas Pinckney might have hoped that the major outbreak of marronage on the Savannah River would be the only such incidence during his governorship, but he was to be disappointed. Only three months after the destruction of the maroon camps on the Savannah River, Pinckney was forced to order out the militia against more maroons, this time encamped near Stono.

3.27] *The governor acts on reports of further maroon activity*

Monday August 6, 1787[1]

His Excellency read a letter dated the 1st instant which he had received from Mr. William Drayton, giving information of a number of runaway Negroes in the neighborhood of Stono and many of them armed.

The Council were of opinion that Col. Vanderhorst, who commands the Berkley County Militia, should be directed to order out a part of the regiment in the vicinity of Rantowles and Stono, for the purpose of breaking up the said party of runaway Negroes.

Charleston, 8th August 1787
Colonel Arnoldus Vanderhorst,
Berkley County Militia

Sir, Having received information that a party of runaway Negro men, many of whom are armed, are become very troublesome, and dangerous to the plantations in the vicinity of Stono, and it being represented that they are too numerous to be quelled by the usual parties of patrol, you will be pleased to order a command from your regiment of such part of the militia of the neighborhood as you may judge sufficient effectually to apprehend or disperse such slaves as fall within the above description.

T[homas] P[inckney]

August 18, 1787

His Excellency requested the advice of Council respecting the arrangement of the militia, especially the lower regiments which have no officers, having received information that the runaway Negroes had in some part of the country become very troublesome.

Recommended that his Excellency should send to the representatives residing in the different parishes or to the commanding offices where there are any of the Militia, requiring the Militia to comply with the late Governor's notification published in _____ and that they accordingly do proceed to make a choice of their officers agreeable thereto on or before the first of October next ensuing.

1. Edwards, ed., *Journals of the Privy Council,* 203–4.

A (Relatively) Peaceful Interlude, 1787–1812

CHAPTER FOUR

There is little evidence for marronage for the thirty years after the major battles between the maroons on the Savannah River and the state militias of South Carolina and Georgia. It is not immediately clear why this is the case since, judging from runaway notices placed in local newspapers, slaves continued to flee from bondage throughout this period. One might imagine that the Haitian revolution, begun by slaves in the summer of 1791, would have inspired copycat actions on the North American mainland, and indeed there is some evidence that both Virginia and North Carolina experienced an upsurge of maroon activity in the 1790s.[1] There were rumors that South Carolina's slaves were plotting an insurrection with counterparts in Virginia in late 1793, and suspicion for a time fell on the French consul in Charleston, but ultimately no concrete evidence was found to corroborate them. Fears that white refugees from Haiti were bringing in potentially seditious slaves eventually led the South Carolina legislature to impose restrictions on the importation of both slaves and free blacks from French islands, but marronage, at least as far as the surviving records tell us, actually became less frequent.[2]

The various plots and rebellions in Virginia at the start of the nineteenth century, although contemporary to the documents in this chapter, also seem not to have been a contributing factor.[3] While it is certainly possible that South Carolina slaves heard of Gabriel Prosser, there is no evidence that they tried to emulate him. Nevertheless, it is hard to imagine that no maroon groups formed in South Carolina between 1787 and 1812 since the lowcountry's swamps retained their allure as potential safe havens. Perhaps maroons became more adept at hiding from white eyes, and from the brief glimpses of maroon activity that do exist in the written record, it seems clear that they did not entirely disappear. In 1788 Charleston Neck had a reputation as being "extremely convenient a place of refuge for runaway negroes, &c. to commit thefts and robberies both in and out of the city," and four years later the Charleston Grand Jury continued to complain about "the number of runway Negroes" and recommended "that the most speedy and effectual measures should be taken to disperse the several gangs we here complain of."[4] As the notice seeking a runaway slave placed by slave owner Arthur Hughes makes clear (document 4.1), some maroons continued to survive for several years in relatively close proximity to Charleston. The impact that the maroons were having in the neighborhood by 1800 was serious enough that the governor ordered military action against them (document 4.2).

1. Frey, *Water from the Rock,* 228–32.
2. Robert Alderson, "Charleston's Rumored Slave Revolt of 1793," in *The Impact of the Haitian Revolution in the Atlantic World,* ed. David P. Geggus (Columbia: University of South Carolina Press, 2001), 93–111; Egerton, *He Shall Go Out Free,* 42–46.
3. Douglas R. Egerton, "Gabriel's Conspiracy and the Election of 1800," *Journal of Southern History* 56 (May 1990): 191–214; Douglas R. Egerton, *Gabriel's Rebellion: The Virginia Slave Conspiracies of 1800 and 1802* (Chapel Hill: University of North Carolina Press, 1993).
4. *Charleston City Gazette,* June 13, 1788; South Carolina Grand Jury presentments, 1792, no. 3, South Carolina Archives.

4.1] *Advertisement of runaway by Arthur Hughes, March 5, 1800*[1]

500 Dollars Reward

ABSENTED themselves from the subscriber, the following Negroes, viz.

TOM, on the 23rd January ult. from the city of Charleston; he is about 42 years of age, of a black complexion, speaks good English, a little knock-kneed, and had on when he went away an iron on one leg, and another on his neck.[2]

CYRUS, from Chehaw, in the month of August last past. He is about five feet six of eight inches high, speaks good English, about 38 years of age, well made, and is remarkable bow legged.

Also, HERCULES, from Chehaw, in the month of February, 1797. He is about five feet eight or nine inches high, stout and well made, speaks good English, is about 36 years old, has remarkable thick lips, and has a small impediment in his speech when frightened, and of a yellowish complexion.

The above three Negroes are harboured on the Ashley River, where TOM and HERCULES had been for three years past, and are now between Wappoo-cut and Ashley River.

One hundred dollars will be paid on conviction of a white person taking, or having taken Tom's irons off, and twenty if by a negro. Also fifty dollars will be paid on delivery of him to the master of the work house; fifty dollars will also be paid on delivery of CYRUS, and one hundred for HERCULES; and further reward of two hundred dollars will be paid on conviction of their being harboured by a white person.

Arthur Hughes
February 15.

1. *City Gazette and Daily Advertiser,* March 5, 1800.
2. Such chains are an indication that Tom was a habitual runaway.

4.2] *Gov. John Drayton writes to Hon. Brig. Gen. Arnold Vanderhorst*[1]

Charleston Sept 5th 1800,
Dear Sir,

In consequence of information given me by Lieut Dupont, respecting armed runaway Negroes in Goose Greek parish (some of whom have already been killed) and influenced by the effect which the ordinance of the City council will have respecting badges, in driving from the City many runaways who are now in it, all of whom will probably harbour, on, or about the neck between Ashley & Cooper Rivers; and also by the representation of Captain George, who states the duty, which he & his company now perform on the neck to be uncommonly fatiguing; I have thought proper to relieve him at different times by a patrole from the city. I therefore request you immediately issue orders to Lieut Col. Commington, directing him to order a troop of horse, once a fortnight to mount guard in the night from 8 oclk at night, until day break: their duty to be to patrole from this city by the different roads to the forks of Ashley ferry & Goose Creek road: to take up all negroes whom they may find, from their homes without tickets, which negroes they are to bring to town, and loose in the workhouse, them to be dealt with according to law.

1. Executive journal of Gov. John Drayton, 114, South Carolina Archives.

In 1800 a Philadelphia newspaper printed a somewhat confused report of a large group of maroons and the governor's decision to send a troop of light horse cavalry against them (document 4.3). Nothing about this group or about the outbreak of yellow fever was printed in the South Carolina papers.

4.3] *Northern newspaper report of an insurrection, 1800*[1]

Extract of a letter from a gentleman in Charleston, [S.C.] to his friend in this city, dated Sept. 13.

"I have just recovered from a severe attack of the yellow fever. It has been very fatal among the northern people—The principal part of those who have taken it have fallen victims.

The negroes have rose in arms against the whites in this country, and have killed several. All the troops of Light Horse are ordered out by the Governor to suppress the insurrection under the penalty of 15 pounds sterling, for every private, and in proportion for the officers. It is expected there will be serious work before they are subdued."

In addition to the above, we leaven by a gentleman from Charleston, that this insurrection had caused a very serious alarm in that city. Some reports stated the number of insurgents, who were embodied about 30 miles from the city, to be about four or five thousand strong. Others decreased this number to 7 or 8 hundred. However this may be, the citizens were unfortunately backward in turning out, owing to the sickly state of the surrounding country. Many chose rather to pay the penalty than run the risk of falling a prey to the fever which generally attacks those inhabitants of Charleston that venture into the country in the autumnal months.

1. *Philadelphia Gazette,* September 23, 1800. This was reprinted in numerous other newspapers in New England over the ensuing weeks. See, for instance, the *Salem Impartial Register,* September 29, 1800; and the *New London Bee,* October 1, 1800.

We can be sure that the blacksmith Adam Culiatt died while hunting runaways (document 4.5), even though a newspaper obituary attributes his demise to a riding accident (document 4.4).

4.4] *Newspaper report of Adam Culiatt's death*[1]

Died, on Wednesday the 15th October, 1800, Mr. Adam Culliatt, of Jacksonborough, the thirty-first year of his age. His death was occasioned by his horse running away with him and violently rushing against a cotton scaffold; he languished about two hours, and was sensible to his end. His funeral was attended by a number of respectable inhabitants, and detachment of the Pon-Pon troop of horse, to which he belonged, and was by them buried, with the honors of war, at the burial ground of his ancestors, on Pon-Pon neck.

1. *Charleston City Gazette,* October 21, 1800.

4.5] *Petitions of Ava Culiatt and Major Brown*

The humble Petition of Ava Culliatt, widow of Adam Culliatt, late of St Paul's parish, blacksmith[1]

Sheweth

That, her said deceased husband being a trooper in the Jacksonborough troop of horse, commanded by Captain Paul Hamilton, was on the fifteenth day of October last ordered out in a detachment of the said troop, under the immediate command of the said Captain, in pursuit of a party of Negro slaves, who had infested that neighbourhood and had recently committed a murder there.

That your petitioner's said husband was while on that service, unfortunately killed by his horse, whereby your petitioner and her infant child are deprived of their only support.

Report of the Assembly Committee

That they have investigated the allegations contained therein, & find the same to be true, & that the Petitioner, is entitled to be provided for by law & recommend the prayer of said petition be granted by allowing the widow a pension of five pds per year during her widowhood, and the like sum of five pds per annum to her only child until it arrives to the age of 12 years, should it live to that time

December 8, 1800. Agreed to December 15, 1800

To the honorable the House of Representatives of the State of South Carolina met in session of 1800—

The humble petition of Major Brown, widow of Joseph Chandler Brown, late of St. Paul's Parish overseer—[2]

Sheweth

That, her said husband did on the fifth day of October last go together with William Dunn, a neighbouring overseer, in search of a gang of runaway negroes the property of divers persons, not living in that neighbourhood—and who infested that part of the country, then very thinly inhabited by white inhabitants. That, said negroes did fire guns at her said husband, & the said William Dunn, by which means her husband was killed on the spot & said Dunn desperately wounded.

That your petitioner, together with small children, the oldest not thirteen years of age, are now reduced to the utmost distress as the labor of the deceased man was their only support.

That, confiding in the legallity of her claim, as sanctioned by the eighth paragraph of the Act for the better Ordering & Governing Negroes, but yet more on the justice & humanity of this Honorable House.

Your petitioner humbly prays this Honorable House, to take her and her four small orphans' case into consideration and to give them such relief therein, as the said Act contemplates, and to this Honorable House shall seem meet.

And your petitioner shall for ever pray.

Major Brown + her mark

December 2, 1800.

Report of the Assembly Committee:

That they have investigated the allegations contained therein, & find the same to be true, & that the Petitioner, is entitled to be provided for by law & considering the importance of encouraging persons to put in execution the Negroe laws of this state, they recommend, that a pension of five pds be allowed annually to the widow during her widowhood, and a sum of five pds per annum to each of the children till they respectively arrive to the age of twelve years, if they shall so long live.

December 19, 1800.

1. South Carolina General Assembly petitions, 1800, no. 167, General Assembly committee reports, microfilm series 108092, reel 29, frame 361, South Carolina Archives.

2. South Carolina General Assembly petitions, 1800, no. 166, General Assembly committee reports, microfilm series 108092, reel 14, frame 452, South Carolina Archives.

The Final Flourishing of Marronage, 1813–1829

CHAPTER FIVE

The period of relative calm after 1787 abruptly ended in the second decade of the nineteenth century as the incidence of marronage grew markedly, climaxing in the early 1820s before gradually fading away. Just as in the decades on both sides of the American Revolution, the appearance of a powerful potential ally, this time in the shape of Great Britain during the War of 1812, perhaps encouraged slaves to flee bondage and form maroon communities. The Charleston newspapers were full of reports on the activities of the British fleet in Chesapeake Bay between February and September 1813, and there were rumors of British warships just offshore.[1] It is hard to imagine that slaves were ignorant of these developments since they would have been popular topics of conversation in the dining rooms and parlors of South Carolinian slaveholders. Perhaps some slaves believed that the British would invade the South as they had done in 1778, and certainly a restless slave population was in British interests.[2] There is, however, no definite evidence linking increased maroon activity to the War of 1812.

The Colleton District Grand Jury complained about the activities of armed runaways in St. Bartholomew's Parish in 1813 (most likely in the swamps surrounding the Ashepoo River or its tributaries, which dominate the geography of the parish), and the Assembly responded by offering to pay "necessary expenses" involved in their capture (document 5.1). Grand Juries were drawn from among the adult white male voters, and as a result in coastal South Carolina they were dominated by slaveholders. Grand Jury presentments permitted the community to give official voice to their concerns and required state or local authorities to formulate a response. This particular presentment suggests that many local residents were aware of the activities of maroons in the district and that at least some maroons were skilled boatmen.

South Carolina law directed that compensation should be paid to slave owners if their slaves were executed by the state after due judicial process. This was to discourage slave owners from protecting felons in order to avoid a financial loss. Fugitive slaves killed by patrols or by the militia were not covered by this compensation package because these executions had not been ordered by the state. This did not prevent slave owners from petitioning the state legislature for recompense when their slaves died in this manner. In documents 5.2 and 5.3 a slaveholder petitions for compensation for a runaway slave killed by the local militia, which had been called out in response to the Grand Jury's presentment. While such petitions were primarily intended to establish legal cause why slaveholders should be compensated by the state, this particular one also reveals more details about white attitudes toward maroons. Specifically, it is clear that the militia operated a shoot-on-sight policy, perhaps indicative of their own perception of the threat posed by the maroons. This slaveholder petitioned twice, in 1814 and again in 1819, and neither time was he successful.

1. For rumors relating to St. Simons Island in Georgia, see the *Savannah Republican*, October 14, 1813. The Charleston authorities passed new regulations to prevent local fishermen from communicating with the British; see *Charleston City Gazette*, June 2, 1813. In July 1813 some northern newspapers (see, for instance, the *Boston Daily Advertiser*, July 8, 1813) printed a report of an insurrection in Hanover, South Carolina, that had involved the massacre of three to four hundred whites and a pitched battle between twelve hundred slaves and nine thousand state troops. Charleston was reported to be in "great confusion . . . in consequence of the above alarming intelligence." However, it is highly unlikely that this report was true. There is no mention of this insurrection in South Carolina's newspapers, and while papers were sometimes reluctant to publish details of slave revolts for fear of encouraging other slaves to revolt, it would be hard to completely cover up such a violent event. Significantly there were no follow-up articles in newspapers in other states that did not have the same fears as those in South Carolina. There is also no evidence that there was a draft for nine thousand state troops or that Charleston was in a state of panic. A final point of doubt must arise from the location of the insurrection—Hanover. As far as I can determine, there was no place of that name in South Carolina in 1813.

2. British admiral Cochrane even issued a statement in April 1814 promising freedom to slaves who joined the British; see Admiral Cochrane's statement, April 2, 1814, ADM 1/508, 579, U.K. National Archives.

5.1] *Grand Jury presentment from Colleton District, November 1813, and the General Assembly's response*[1]

Presentment:
We present as a grievance the numerous assemblies of armed runaway slaves incamped within said district to the great annoyance of the inhabitants thereof; and to the even rendering of the navigation of the rivers and creeks therein

excessively dangerous, owing to the depredations of this Banditti furnished as they are with boats thereon.

Response:

Your committee further recommend that a sum be appropriated for defraying the expenses that may be necessary in apprehending and dispersing the armed Negroes runaway In said District.

1. South Carolina General Assembly Grand Jury presentments, 1783–1877: 1813, no. 2, General Assembly, Judiciary Committee, report on the presentments of the Grand Jury of Colleton District, series S165005, 1813, no. 25, South Carolina Archives.

5.2] *Matthew O'Driscoll petitions for compensation*[1]

To the Honorable the President and the other Honorable Members of the Senate of the State of South Carolina met in Session of 1814.

The Humble Petition of Matthew O'Driscoll[2] Sheweth

That two very valuable slaves the property of your Petitioner were shot dead, by an armed party during his late attendance on a committee of the House of Representatives on charges of misconduct in Office as Clerk, Ordinary and Register of Colleton District brought against him by Hugh McBurney.

That the said party was commanded by Lieutenant Ford now a member of the Honorable the House of Representatives and the act by them attempted to be justified on the ground of these Slaves being runaways from the service of their Owner and that they were justified in killing them by virtue of a clause in the Militia Law passed the 10th day of May 1804,[3] which they aver specifies that such party has the legal right to kill any slave "that shall have absented himself from the service of his owner and shall flee from pursuit."

That your Petitioner's slaves were not accused of having committed any overt act or injured any person during their absence from him, and that he alone was thereby a sufferer; he therefore presumes that if policy should require and induce the Legislature of his Country to pass a law, which thus deprived him of his property, it will reimburse him to the full amount of the loss which he has sustained.

That your petitioner is the more assured of this as he knows it to be a standing Rule of your Honorable House, and sanctioned by law to pay a certain proportion of their value even to the owners of slaves, whose lives have been forfeited by the sentence of a Court of Justices for crimes which affect the Public and render them unfit to live.

That this very case furnishes this strong instance, which induces your Petitioner to hope for relief. At the time his negroes were shot they were accompanied by a negro slave named April, the property of Thomas W. Price this slave, a noted public offender then escaped but was since taken, tried, convicted and executed for crimes of which he was then guilty, and his owner is now intitled to the usual remuneration from your Honorable House, and will apply for it, tho' his life was forfeited not by its interference or by any immediate injunction from it.

Your Petitioner therefore prays your Honorable House for such relief as to its wisdom & justice may seem meet.

Matthew O'Driscoll.

1. South Carolina General Assembly petitions, 1814, no. 119, South Carolina Archives.
2. According to the 1810 census, O'Driscoll owned twenty slaves in Colleton District.
3. The militia was authorized to take "such measures to suppress such insurrections ... [as] shall appear most proper & effectual" (an act to organize the militia throughout the state of South Carolina, May 10, 1794, in *Acts of the General Assembly of the State of South Carolina* [Columbia, S.C.: D. & J. J. Faust, state printers, 1808], 1:312). O'Driscoll misdates this law in his petition.

5.3] *Matthew O'Driscoll petitions again for compensation*[1]

To the Honorable the Speaker and Members of the House of Representatives.

The Memorial of Dr Matthew O'Driscoll of the city of Charleston, late of Saint Bartholomew's Parish.

Shewith, that some years ago, to wit, in the year 1813, he was owner of two negro fellow slaves named Brister & Gabriel, who ran away from him & were harboured by some of their acquaintances, on a certain plantation, in the said Parish of St Bartholomews. That, a detachment of Militia, by an act of assembly passed the 10th day of May 1794, was ordered out to disperse, suppress, kill, destroy, apprehend, take or subdue the said slaves. That the said Detachment of Militia, arriving at the plantation where the said slaves were suspected to be lurking, and upon their fleeing, the said Detachment immediately shot them down and killed them. That, thereby, the loss of your memorialist has been very considerable. The value of the said Fellow Brister, being at least $600 that of the fellow Gabriel, at the least $400, and from that time a period of six years, your memorialist has not only been deprived of the services of said slaves, but has been out of even the legal interest on their value.

And your memorialist further shewith, that presuming at the time that the said Act, on the part of the Detachment of Militia, was justifyable & was authorised by law, in the year 1814—he submitted the circumstances of his case through a memorial to your Honorable body, praying remuneration at the hands of the state. That a committee of one Honorable body reported in favor of your memorialist, while the House of Representatives thought proper at that time to reject the application, on the ground, as your memorialist is informed and believes, that serious doubts were entertained by the House, whether the Law, under which the said Detachment of Militia acted, would justify the measures they took, and the extremities to which they went, and required, before they would consent to the granting of your memorialist any relief, that your memorialist should take proper measures to have the same determined by the decision of some judicial tribunal.

That in compliance with this view of that Honorable body, your memorialist commenced and prosecuted his action at Law, against the parties implicated; and at a Court of Common Pleas, held at Jacksonborough, for Colleton District, on the 16th day of April, A.D. 1819, before the Honorable Judge Johnson, the jury returned a special Verdict, in these words, to wit "We find that the negroes Bristol[2] and Gabriel the property of Dr Matthew O'Driscoll, were lawfully killed, by a party of Militia, assembled under the proper officers, and acting according to the provision, of the act of 1794. And we therefore find a Verdict for the Defendant" a certified copy of which Verdict, is herewith respectfully submitted.

And your memorialist, here respectfully brings to the view of your Honorable body that his said slaves, had been guilty of no offence, except against your memorialist; and that only in the venial offence of running away from his employ. That certainly without any fault or neglect on the part of your memorialist, the lives of his slaves have been taken away, and his property destroyed under the sanction of the law of the state, which, by the construction it has received, deprives your memorialist of any private redress, at the hands of those engaged in the said transaction: by a law which must ever operate unequally on the Citizens at large, and which as in this instance, has operated in a manner unforeseen, and, even never contemplated by the Legislature itself. That, under the operation of this law; such like property of no man may be considered safe, and however vigilant the citizens be, ruin may await him, when he least suspects it.

That the facts, as in the above Verdict, being thus solemnly established, your memorialist again submits his case to the consideration of your Honorable Body, and prays, that compensation may be allowed him by the state, for the loss of his said slaves, and the expenses he has incurred in prosecuting his said action at Law. And your memorialist as in duty bound will ever pray and so forth.

M^w O'Driscoll
November 15th 1819.

1. South Carolina General Assembly petitions, 1819, no. 109 (verbatim copy to the Senate, no. 110), South Carolina Archives. The House of Representatives Committee on Claims recommended refusal, which was agreed to by the House on December 15, 1819 (Committee on Claims reports, series S165005, 1819, no. 183, South Carolina Archives).

The Senate Committee on Claims, on the other hand, recommended that O'Driscoll be allowed the normal compensation for executed slaves, which, with costs, amounted to $431.72. The Senate initially accepted the report on December 17, 1819, but on learning two days later of the House's decision to refuse the claim, "resolved that they do disagree to the report," and therefore it seems that O'Driscoll received nothing (Committee on Claims reports, series S165005, 1819, no. 184, South Carolina Archives).

2. O'Driscoll clearly wrote "Brister" when referring to this individual earlier in his memorial, but the jury used the more familiar slave name of "Bristol."

Like Matthew O'Driscoll, the planter Edward Brailsford[1] *twice sought compensation for two "valuable" slaves killed by a patrol that was hunting a gang of runaways near Goose Creek. Although the second petition is not dated, it seems likely, given the dating evidence in the House of Assembly records, that it was from 1822. It should be recalled that Denmark Vesey's conspiracy was still fresh in the minds of South Carolinians in late December 1822 when Brailsford's second petition was being considered, and this may have been a factor in the decision to refuse it.*

1. In the 1820 census Mrs. Brailsford, perhaps Edward's widow, owned nine slaves in Charleston District.

5.4] Edward Brailsford seeks compensation for slaves killed by patrols hunting runaways

State of South Carolina[1]

To the Honorable the Speaker and Members of the House of Representatives of the State of South Carolina

The humble petition of Edward Brailsford

Respectfully Sheweth.

That your petitioner was the owner of two slaves called Cyrus and Absolum, the first about 22 the latter about 27 years of age. That the said negroes were both *stout, prime, healthy* and *valuable* negroes and field hands. That in March 1814 your petitioner hired his said two slaves to a certain Captn Brandt, who planted on Long Island in the State aforesaid. That whilst the said slaves remained with your petitioner they conducted themselves well and he had no fault to find with them, but from some cause unknown to your petitioner the said slaves in the summer of 1814 ran away from the said Captn Brandt and went & remained in the neighbourhood of your petitioner's plantation in St James Parish, Goose Creek about 16 miles from the City of Charleston. That your petitioner was then residing in the City of Charleston. That in the fall and winter of 1814 there was a Gang of Run away Negroes who were so very troublesome and offensive in that neighbourhood and about Dorchester as to induce the inhabitants to turn out with a view to apprehend them. That it was reported and believed (but on what grounds your petitioner is ignorant) that the two slaves above mentioned formed a part of this Gang. That the patroles had positive orders if they met with any of the said Gang & they would not stop and surrender themselves to shoot them down. And your petitioner further shews unto your Honorable Body that a Patrole under the command, he believes, of Captain Prior and on public duty and charged with the orders aforesaid surprised at night on your petitioners plantation the fellow Absolum, who had gone there for their purpose of seeing his wife who belonged to your petitioner & was then staying at his plantation. That the said fellow Absolum ran out of the negro house in which he was, and was endeavouring to make his escape when he was fired at by the patrole & killed.

That a few days afterwards the other fellow Cyrus was surprised by the patrole in the neighbourhood of Dorchester and as he was endeavoring to make his escape, he was fired at and likewise killed.

Your petitioner begs leave further to state that the said slaves were young, strong, healthy & very valuable negroes. That during the time they remained with your petitioner they never misbehaved themselves, but on the contrary always conducted themselves with great propriety. That by their death your petitioner has sustained a considerable loss and as they were killed by persons vested with authority by the state and for the public Good, he humbly conceives that he is entitled to a remuneration for his said losses from your honorable Body.

Your petitioner therefore prays your Honorable Body to take his case into consideration & that you would be pleased to order and direct such an amount to be paid to your petitioner as you should deem a sufficient recompense for his losses and that you would please to grant to him such further & other relief as to your Honorable Body shall seem meet.

And your petitioner as in duty bound will every pray and so forth
Ed. Brailsford
Sworn before me this 26th day of November 1816.
Lewis Roux

Charleston Novem^r 27th 1816 [2]
Dear Sir

I now do myself the pleasure of transmitting to you, by my friend Mr Mann, this letter relating to a petition drawn out by Mr Parker, my attorney, concerning two valuable young fellows of mine, who were shot by the patrol, on public duty, in St. George's, as expressed in said petition.—I cannot but think that I should be remunerated for this serious loss—a great loss to me as an individual, & is very sensibly felt.

I am truly opinion that every planter is deeply interested, & should be for a remuneration, as their property is sometimes exposed to similar dangers, &

the like may occur again on your or any other plantation. Where an individual's property falls a sacrifice to public orders, & for public benefit, it is no more than just & right, that he should be amply compensated for the loss sustained.—These were valuable field hands, hostler & plough-man, & capable of doing any work on a plantation.—Let me request of you, therefore, to exert yourself on my behalf, and to get it passed through the house, so as to fulfill my expectations.—Your compliance will oblige, Dear Sir, yours with esteem & respect

E^d Brailsford.
To Daniel Ravenel Esqr
Representative
Columbia
S^o C^a

1. South Carolina General Assembly petitions, 1816, no. 100, South Carolina Archives.
2. South Carolina General Assembly, series S165029, 1816, item 4, South Carolina Archives.

5.5] *Edward Brailsford tries again in 1822*[1]

State of South Carolina
To the Honorable the Speaker and Members of the House of Representatives,

The humble petition of Edward Brailsford of the City of Charleston, and State aforesaid, respectfully sheweth.

That your Petitioner's planting interest, in St James's Goose Creek, being near a body of run away negroes, who had become very offensive to the parishioners in that neighbourhood and who had enticed two of your Petitioner's primest fellows to join them, and were becoming daily more and more offensive to all in the vicinity of that place, repeatedly committing depredations on their property, the Capt of the Parish was ordered to summon a body of men to patrole the Country, for the express purpose of pursuing, taking, or firing upon such as would not surrender. In pursuance of these orders some were routed in the vicinity of Dorchester, when Cyrus, the property of your petitioner was shot, and killed. Some were routed within the limits of your petitioner's plantation, when Absolum was shot, and soon after expired. These two fellows were the property of your petitioner, and were young, and athletick and truly valuable fellows. Your petitioner, therefore, humbly prayeth, that your Honorable House will take into consideration the loss experienced on this occasion, in the death of these two prime young fellows, for the good of the community, and that your petitioner may be amply remunerated for the loss of property thus sustained, and now sensibly felt.

And your Petitioner, as in duty bound, will ever pray.
Edward Brailsford

The special committee to whom were referred the Petition of Edward Brailsford praying compensation for certain slaves killed by a Patrole or detatchment of the Militia in pursuit of Runaways, report that the prayer of the Petition ou[gh]t not to be granted said slaves being in a state of actual rebellion.

P. Moser Chair^m

Decr 12th 1822[2]

1. South Carolina General Assembly, petition ND, no. 1837, marked on back "rejected." This petition was read in the House on December 12, 1822, and referred to the Committee on Claims (House of Representatives, 1822, South Carolina Archives).

2. South Carolina General Assembly, series S165005, 1822, item 156, South Carolina Archives. This report was read in the House on December 14, 1822, and was ordered to be reconsidered. A second committee agreed with the original decision. See South Carolina General Assembly, series S165005, 1822, item 157, South Carolina Archives.

In his annual message to the General Assembly in 1816 (document 5.6) Gov. David Williams reported that he had authorized military action against maroons in Colleton District. It is possible that these maroons were the same group as those complained about by the Grand Jury in 1813 (document 5.1) since Williams notes that they had been there "for a long time," and indeed these swamps had been popular as far back as 1765. The second undated source (document 5.7) makes reference to Williams's action and was likely written in either 1816 or 1817. It gives further information about the activities of these maroons and others who used the man-made "cuts" between rivers to navigate their way from swamp to swamp.

5.6] *Gov. David Williams's annual message to the General Assembly, November 24, 1816*[1]

Two events have occurred, during the present year, which required a resort to military force.[2] A few runaway negroes, concealing themselves in the swamps and marshes contiguous to Combahee and Ashepoo rivers, not having been interrupted in their petty plunderings for a long time, formed the nucleus, round which, all the ill-disposed and audacious near them gathered, until at length their robberies became too serious to be suffered with impunity. Attempts were then made to disperse them, which either from insufficiency of numbers, or bad arrangement, served by their failure only to encourage a wanton destruction of property. Their force now became alarming, not less from its numbers, than from its arms and ammunition, with which it was supplied. The peculiar situation of the whole of that portion of our coast, rendered access to them difficult, while the numerous creeks and water sources through the marshes and round the islands, furnished them easy opportunities to plunder, not only the planters in open day, but the inland coasting trade also, without leaving a trace of their movements by which they could be pursued. There was but one more stage, to a state of things, altogether intolerable; to prevent which, I felt it my duty to use the public force and the public money. I therefore ordered Colonel, now Major General Wm. Youngblood,[3] to take the necessary measures for suppressing them, and authorized him to incur the customary expenses of such an expedition. This was immediately executed. By a judicious employment of the militia under his command, he either captured, or destroyed, the whole body. As the amount of the expenses authorized, has not yet been ascertained, and of course not paid, I ask of the legislature to put at the disposal of my successor, a sum adequate to redeem my promise.

1. *Message No 1. from the Governor of South-Carolina, delivered to both branches of the Legislature. 26th Nov. 1816* (printed copy in the South Carolina Archives; also printed in the *Charleston City Gazette,* December 6, 1816).

2. The other event, not included here, was an insurrection plot by slaves in Camden, which was betrayed by another slave before it began.

3. Youngblood was promoted on March 25, 1816 (*Charleston City Gazette,* April 1, 1816), strongly suggesting that this expedition against the maroons occurred in early 1816.

5.7] *Petition of local residents about the use by maroons of man-made "cuts" between rivers*[1]

To the Honble President and Members of the Senate State of South Carolina

The Humble and Respectful Petition of the Subscribers Sheweth—That on the 15th of September 1779 an act was passed "To cut, sink, clear and keep clear and in repair, a Cut from Ashepoo to Pon-Pon[2] River &c &c, to be not over (30) thirty feet in breadth and (8) Eight feet deep, and that all male persons from 16 to 60 making use of or residing on any Landing on the Ashepoo or any of its Branches thereof (all of the Islands below said cut excepted) shall personally work in cutting &c &c, or to be assessed three days notice, or refusal £3 per day for each"—Grimke's Laws page 304, published 1790.

And whereas said Cut has not within present recollection been opened or worked by the persons liable according to Law and is now about two feet wide and in places not so deep and is seldom if ever used but by Runaways and Negroes unlawfully trading from River to River—During the late war of 1812 with England the number and depredations on Plantations and Rivers of Runaways & Outlaws was so great residing on the Margins and impregnable Fastness of this Negro thoroughfare surrounded by an immense swamp of impregnable and uninhabited marsh and Yi Yi, as to induce Govr D. R. Williams to order out a detatchment of Militia under Col Youngblood which captured with much difficulty the two desperate ringleaders Mowby and Dunmore[3] who with their principal associates, were accordingly executed, to the great relief of the inhabitants adjacent to this cut, and which now remains in its former abandonment and can be only used at extreme high water—at any other time, only by Paddling Boats which at any time can slip through without the aid of water. This cut now prevents the irrigation of a large extent of Land which must ever remain a loss to the State, the Parish and the Owners and continue a Harbour for Runaways and unlawful Negro escape and Traffic as it can never be reclaimed but by fresh water Irrigation and consequently becomes then the Residence of the white Population.

We therefore Humbly Petition your Honble Body that so much of said law as relates to the Cut betwixt Ashepoo & Pon Pon Rivers having become obsolete and a nuisance may be repealed and the same be stopd & discontinued as a public Highway.

Francis Y. Glover on Ashepoo & Pon Pon; Edward Glover Elliotts cut; Wm Lowney Ashepoo; Robert B. Jenkins Ashepoo; Burrell Sanders Ashepoo; Thos G. Skinner Ashepoo; Joseph White Ashepoo River, Henry Ferguson ditto; J. P. Warren do; Wm Eliott of Pon Pon & Ashepoo; Charles S. Minott; S. Purdie on the waters; Joel Linsey Ashepoo; C. Baring farmer, J. M. Cunningham Ashepoo; Henry Hyne Senr Ashepoo; Huskett S. Rhett Ashepoo; S. J. Grant Ashepoo; James Stanfield, John D. Edwards, A. H. Jenkins Ashepoo; Benj^mn Sander; Wm Zom; Wyart B. King

Barnwell Gross Ashepoo; Archd L. Campbell D L Surveyor; Edward Bayard Ashepoo; Tom C. Hazel Pon Pon; Jas Arighton Pon Pon; Jas McPherson Creigton Pon Pon; S. D. Warren Ashepoo; Thos R. S. Elliot do; S. L. Paul Ashepoo; J. Malack ford of the ; S. Prommen; J. P. Allston; H. W. Ford; Josiah Beck; Loftus C. Clifford Pon Pon; Jas M. Rhett Ashepoo; E. Witsell Ashepoo; P. F. Meggeth Ashepoo; Wm W. Seabrook Do; S. E. Seabrook do; W. B. Seabrook do; E. M. Seabrook Ashepoo; J F. Magett Ashepoo; Cavel G. Sanderson Captain of Schooner Magnolia.

1. South Carolina General Assembly, petition ND, no. 2849, South Carolina Archives.
2. Another name for the lower reaches of the Edisto River.
3. It is possible that this was an alias adopted by the maroon leader in memory of Virginia governor Dunmore, whose 1775 proclamation promised freedom to slaves who fought with the British.

A diary entry from the summer of 1819 (document 5.8) tells of an attempt to attack a maroon band hidden in the Santee River swamps near Pineville in the far north of Charleston District, about fifty miles from the coast.

FACING: Detail from "A map of South Carolina and a part of Georgia. Containing the whole sea-coast . . . ," 1780. Courtesy of the Library of Congress, Geography and Map Division

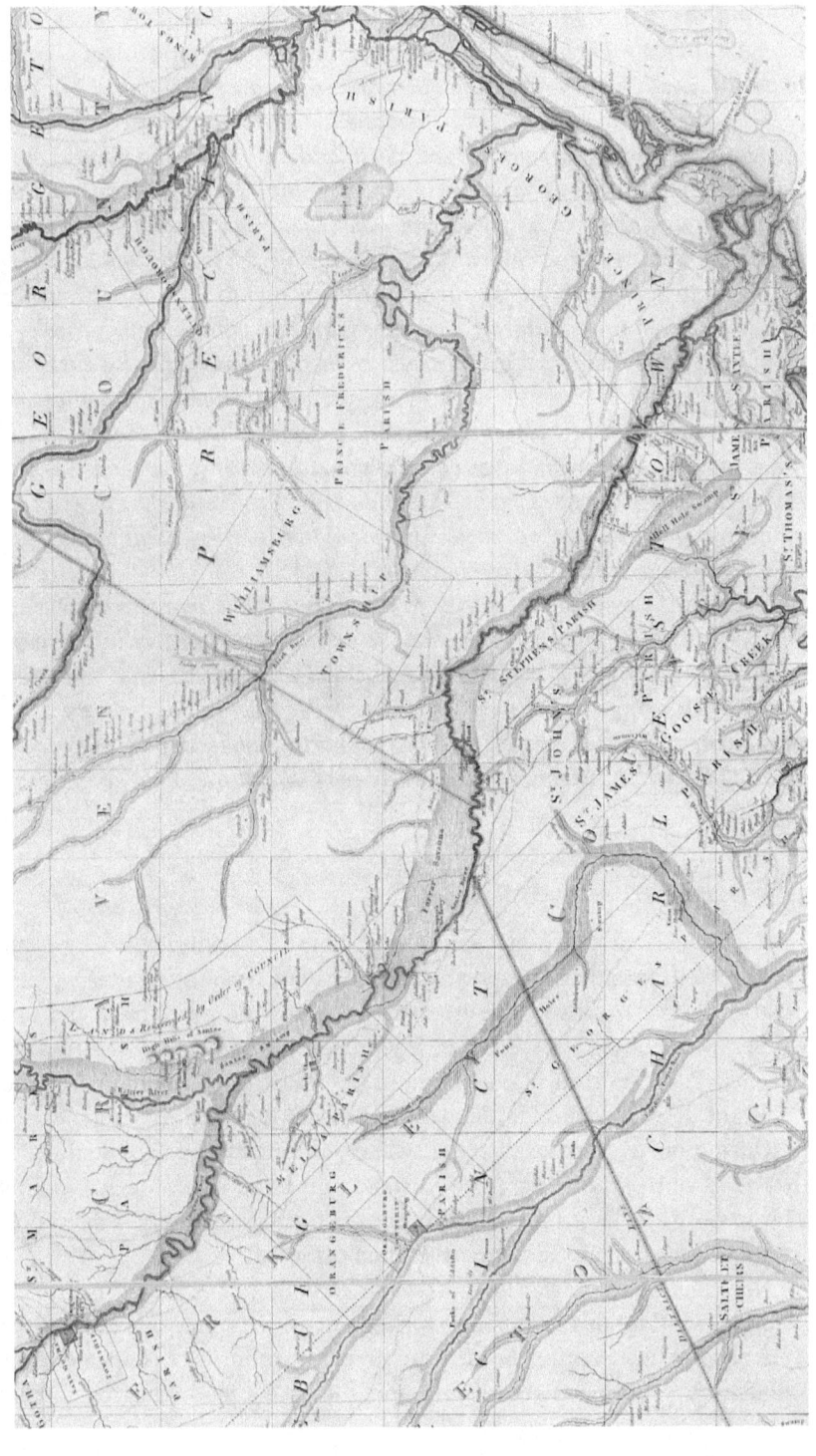

Until the mid-twentieth century the Santee River meandered more for more than a hundred miles inland from its egress into the Atlantic south of Georgetown to its division into the Wateree and Congaree southeast of Columbia. The creation of Lake Marion and Lake Moultrie permanently altered the course of the river, and the Santee is no longer navigable this far inland, but in the nineteenth century it was possible to travel by boat as far inland as Columbia. On both sides of the river extensive swamps stretched for several miles, creating an inhospitable landscape that was unsettled and uncultivated. Roads crossing the swamp and the river from southwest to northeast were few and far between, and roads running roughly parallel to the river, from southeast to northwest, rarely came within five miles of the river. Even today there is little road access to the river, and it remains a true wilderness area. For those enslaved in this part of South Carolina, the Santee swamps offered numerous hiding places that were distant enough from plantations without being totally isolated. The river effectively acted as a highway and was used by maroons along its entire length. The small tributary creeks that flowed into the main river provided easy access to many plantations, where additional food, tools, weapons, and recruits could be obtained.

Document 5.8 gives little clue as to the origins of the maroons, how long they had been there, or what had provoked the military action. More information can be obtained about this group from the petition of yet another planter to the General Assembly seeking compensation for a slave killed during this military operation (document 5.9). David Rodgers included supporting evidence from other local residents along with his claim, but ultimately the General Assembly declined to compensate him.

5.8] *Diary entry of Henry Ravenel*[1]

1819 July 12. A party of Gent^m from PineVille commanded by Major S. Porcher went into the swamp to attack a party of runaway negros supposed to be armed. The squadron consisted of the following gentlemen, Jno and Jo^s Palmer, S. Dubose, Thos Porcher, P. Porcher, I. Porcher, J. E. Cordes, Jno. S Ravenel, T. L Gourdin, S. G. Deveaux, Ja^s & David Gaillard, W. Couturier, J. Dwight, Dr S. Dwight, H. Glendkamp,—Jones & myself.

During our researches thro the swamp, an unfortunate accident occurred, by one of our party firing, (thro mistake supposing him a negro) at another, Tho L. Gourdin, shot J^{as} Gaillard in the foot a slight wound.—We proceeded from Milford down to Richmond[2] & then came out.

N.B. The above party did not see or hear any of runaway negros in the swamp. Two Captains Companies turned out on the other side of the river but were equally unsuccessful. Some time previous to our excursion, a party from Williamsburg patrolled the swamp and shot a couple of negros, a fellow &

wench one belonging to C. Lenud the other owner unknown, both negros died, a few days after our hunt, another party from Williamsburg on a similar hunt shot a fellow of T. Gaillard and took some others armed, amongst them a ringleader, named Billy from the Southward. He gives intelligence of a party of 30 negros most of whom are armed some in Hell-hole Swamp[3] the rest in Santee Swamp, & a regular chain extending towards Georgetown.

 1. Diary of Henry Ravenel, Henry Ravenel Family Papers, South Carolina Historical Society, Charleston, S.C. Henry Ravenel (1790–1867) was a doctor and planter. His Pooshee plantation near the Santee Canal is now submerged underneath Lake Moultrie.
 2. Milford plantation was owned by Isaac Dubose (father of Samuel Dubose), while Richmond plantation was owned by the Palmer brothers. Both were located on Outside Creek adjacent to the swamps on the south side of the Santee in St. Stephen's Parish, Charleston District. The distance between the two was about two miles. See Samuel Dubose, "Reminiscences of St. Stephen's Parish, Craven County and Notices of Her Old Homesteads," in T. Gaillard Thomas, *A Contribution to the History of the Huguenots of South Carolina* (New York: Knickerbocker Press, 1887), 43–45.
 3. In St. James' Santee Parish, Charleston District, between the Cooper and Santee rivers.

5.9] *Petition of David Rodgers and supporting documents*[1]

To the Honorable the President and members of the Senate.

 The Memorial of David L. Rodgers of Williamsburgh District, Respectfully representeth to your honorable body, a loss which he has sustained in getting a prime Negro fellow killed during the summer of 1819. Your memorialist will further state to your honorable body, the particulars of the untimely death of the Negro; which statement will be accompanied with corroborating testimony on the subject. During the Summer of 1819 a pretty large gang, to the number of sevin Negroes[2] had associated and inbodied themselves together, committing depredation of many kinds on the property of the inhabitants. Many attempts were made to detect the said Negroes but all attempts proved abortive for some lapse of time. It was eventually thought to be by the Colonel of the regiment, indispensably necessary that the people should turn out with Fire Arms and quell the Negroes in their nefarious Acts. This last and only probable way, of subduing the Negroes was agreed upon and pursued for some time: Ultimately the negroes were found imbodied and measurably in a state of rebellion, against the peace and welfare of the neighborhood. They manifested in their conduct no pacifick disposition to surrender, when ordered to give up; but endured as far as possible to effect their escape. In doing which, this said negro fellow belonging to your memorialist was shot dead.

 Your memorialist will also state to your honorable body that the said Negro was very valuable in many respects; he was a good boat hand, a very prime field hand; a good sawyer, And was quite handy in the use of Mechanical Tools of different kinds. The said negroe, was between Forty and forty five Years of Age and in all probability would have commanded at the time of being killed, at least nine hundred or one thousand dollars. He had sustained previous to being killed, uniformly, a good character, with the exception of running away once or twice at farthest. Your Memorialist therefore prays, that your honourable Body will in its Philanthropy, and Liberality grant him a remuneration for the loss which he has sustained. And farther, when your honorable Body is informed that your Memorialist is not able to bear with such a loss; he will every pray that you may grant him a compensation.

Nov 21st 1820 David P. Rodgers.[3]

State of South Carolina

Williamsburg District

Personally appeared before me, Joseph Adams, one of the Justices assigned to keep the peace Colonel William Salters and Capt. Issac Nelson who being duly sworn sayeth that in the summer of 1819, they were present the day on which a Negro fellow named Pompey was killed belonging to David L. Rodgers of the District and State aforesaid. They farther state that said Negro Pompey had been in the woods for some time with other Negroes; who had imbodied themselves together against the peace and property of the Citizens of the District. And in order to apprehend said negroes it was thought necessary to go armed; and in taking them the said negro Pompey was killed on the spot. These deponents further say, that he considered said Pompey as valuable as any other Negro of his age in the District of the same occupations.

W. Salters

I. Nelson

Sworn and subscribed before me this 21 day of November 1820

Joseph Adams J. S.

State of South Carolina

Williamsburg District

Personally appeared before me, Joseph Adams, one of the Justices assigned to keep the peace William Frierson Senr of the District and State Aforesaid who being duly sworn sayeth that he raised from a boy, a negro fellow named Pompey, which negro he gave a few years since to David P. Rodgers, as part of a portion in Marriage. And that he the said Wiliam Frierson, considered said Negro Pompey, very valuable in many respects; as being a good Boat hand, a prime field hand; a good sawyer, and handy in the use of Mechanical Tools. The said Negro, he considered between forty and forty five years of age, at the time he was killed.

Wm Frierson

Sworn and subscribed before me this 21 day of November 1820
Joseph Adams J. S.
State of South Carolina
Williamsburg District

Personally appeared before me, Joseph Adams, one of the Justices assigned to keep the peace Ebenezer Gibson of the District and State aforesaid who being duly sworn; sayeth that he knew for a number of years a negro fellow named Pompey belonging to David L. Rodgers; and that he the said Ebenezer Gibson, has had the said negro Pompey frequently in the Boat as a hand; and that he considered said Negroe a valuable boat hand, and also valuable in many other respects.

Eben^r Gibson
Sworn and subscribed before me this 21 day of November 1820
Joseph Adams J. S.

1. South Carolina General Assembly petitions, 1820, no. 144, South Carolina Archives.

2. Since just seven slaves hardly constitute "a pretty large gang," it is possible that this should read "seventy."

3. The Committee on Claims recommended that this petition be refused (report concerning the petition of David P. Rodgers asking compensation for a Negro killed, South Carolina Archives, record series: S165005, 1820, no. 00232, dated November 30, 1820). The House of Representatives agreed with the committee's recommendation on December 1, 1820.

In 1821 a maroon leader named Joe (alias Forest) leaped to prominence in the minds of many white South Carolinians. In May of that year he led a raiding party down the Santee River to George R. Ford's plantation on South Island,[1] and during the course of the raid Ford was killed while trying to protect his property. Ford was neither the first nor the last white person to be killed by maroons: Stephen St. John was "killed by runaway Negroes" in April 1793, and Benjamin O'Bannon was killed in Chester District in 1830 by a maroon group led by "Big George." Yet the reaction to Ford's murder was far greater than reactions to the others' deaths.[2] The reaction can be judged partially from newspaper reports of the event (documents 5.10 and 5.11) and of the hunt, capture, trial, and eventual execution of some of Joe's band. The reward offered by the governor of South Carolina (document 5.12) provides further details, including descriptions of Joe and one of his followers and information about their backgrounds and the various camps they had up and down the river. The governor's reward was claimed by a militia captain (document 5.13). The claim of Meshack Williams (document 5.14) for reimbursement of supplies provided to the militia is evidence of the duration and extent of their searches for Joe. The newspapers followed the hunt for Joe closely (document 5.15) and tried, with varying degrees of success, to keep their readers accurately informed.

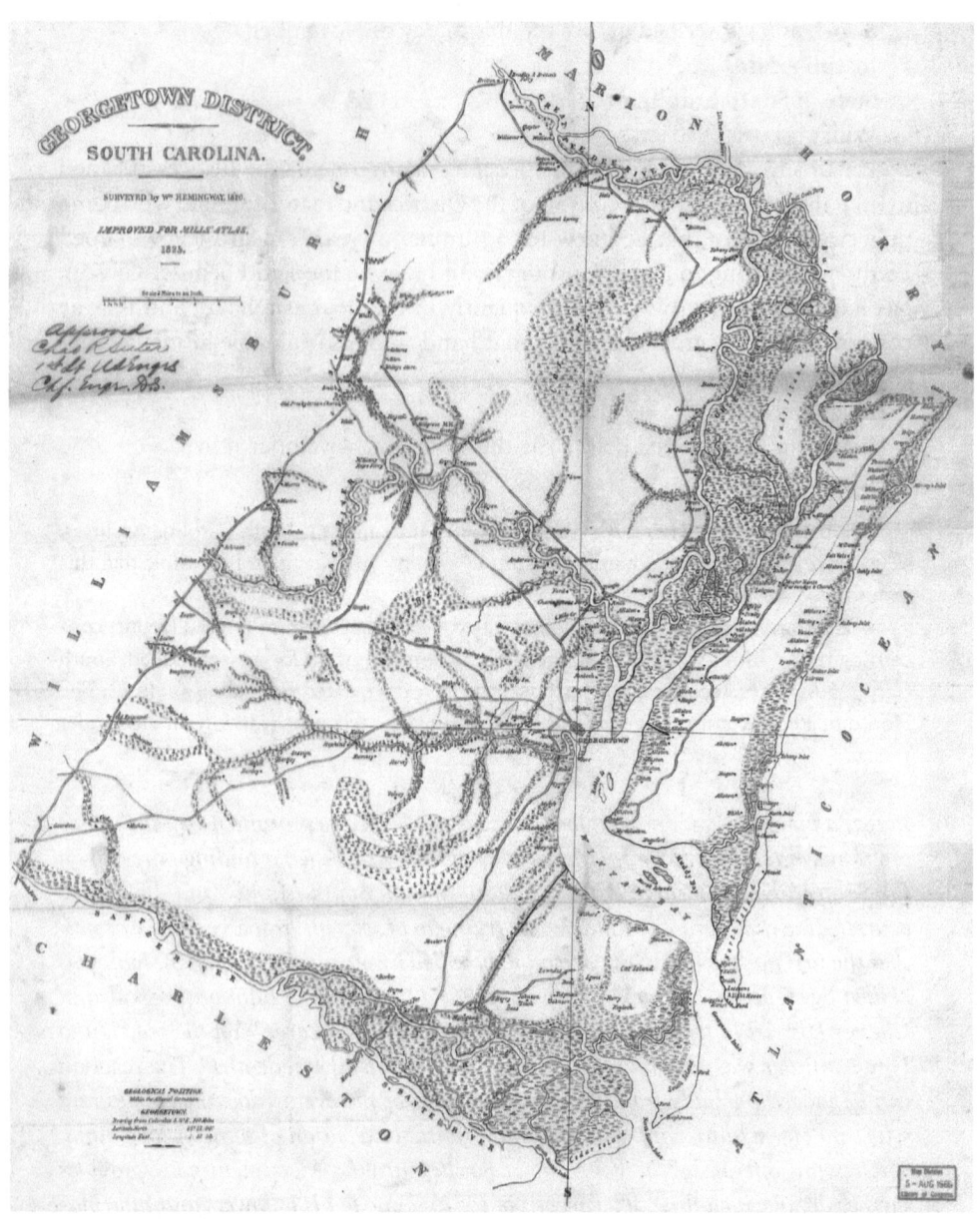

"Georgetown District, South Carolina, surveyed by Wm. Hemingway, 1820; improved for *Mills' Atlas*, 1825." Baltimore: Lucas, 1825. Courtesy of the Library of Congress, Geography and Map Division

1. Ford's Point was located directly opposite a branch of the North Santee River.

2. *Columbian Herald or the Independent Courier of North America,* May 18, 1786; South Carolina General Assembly petitions, 1793, no. 30; *Augusta Chronicle,* November 24, 1830. Forty-one men spent fifteen days hunting runaways after St. John's death; see Herbert Aptheker, "Additional Data on American Maroons," *Journal of Negro History* 32 (October 1947): 454.

5.10] **Newspaper report of the murder of George Ford**[1]

GEORGETOWN, MAY 30

We have to-day to perform the painful duty of announcing the death of GEORGE R. FORD,[2] Esq. a respectable planter of South Island, in this neighborhood. To record the death of so valuable a citizen and so good a man, is at all times an unpleasant task, but it becomes painful in the extreme, when we are compelled, as in the present instance, to add, that he has been suddenly and in the prime of life, snatched from society and the bosom of an affectionate family, by the hand of brutal violence.

On Sunday night last,[3] between the hours of ten and eleven o'clock, Mr. Ford having received information that some negroes were engaged in killing his cattle, he together with one or two of his negroes, and a white man, a carpenter employed by him, went in search of them; the latter carried a gun: They had not proceeded far before a small dog that accompanied them by yelping in an unusual manner, drew the attention of the party, and a noise in the bushes, attracted the notice of Mr. Ford; at this moment a gun was discharged by an unknown hand at Mr. Ford's party, who were immediately dispersed, and the fate of Mr. F. was not known for a considerable time: it appears that the villains after being discovered by Mr. Ford's servants, anticipating his arrival, had advanced about a mile and a half to meet him, and made choice of the most favorable situation for waylaying him, and perpetrating an act on which they had deliberately determined. A faithful fellow in the mean time, armed with a gun, concealed himself behind the ox that had been killed in the hopes to detect them in their attempt to remove it—in this he was not mistaken, and he was fortunate in taking one of these daring villains as he approached. As soon as assistance could be procured, Mr. F. was sought for, and found dead on the spot on which he was shot; the gun had been loaded with slugs, and a ball; the principal part of the slugs entered his head—the ball penetrated his breast; two of the negroes were also wounded—one of them severely near the temple and in the groin.

The fellow, who has been taken is a young negro man, called *Jack,* the property of Mrs. Horry, and from his confession it appears that there were two others engaged with him; they had descended the Santee in a canoe, and entered a small creek which leads from the river into the plantation of Mr. F. He gives the following description of his two companions. *Joe,* their ringleader, is of yellow complexion (but he is not a mulatto), about six feet high, uncommonly stout and well made—he has on one of his cheeks (it is believed on his right cheek) a scar about the size of a quarter of a dollar. He came from the neighborhood of Mr. McCord's ferry.[4] Jack is a short, thick negro, and came from above Columbia, or Camden, and is the fellow who shot Mr. Ford; both of these fellows have been in the neighborhood about five months and are constantly armed. The fellow in custody says he was present when Joe attempted to shoot Mr. McClenan, of Santee. He says that the gun did not snap as reported, but that McClenan's life was saved by the sudden wheeling of his horse, and his precipitate flight. This is the gang who twice fired on white persons on Santee, and have for a length of time committed depredations in that neighborhood.

We feel much gratified in having in our power to state, that since the foregoing account was sent to the press, a detachment of the Washington Greens, under the command of Captain Carnes, have returned to the town, having in their custody, Jack, who is charged with having shot Mr. F. He and his accomplice Joe, and a negroe woman were met by this detachment, a little before daylight yesterday morning[5] and on their refusing to yield, were fired on by one of the men; the woman was wounded, and the men endeavoured to make their escape, when Jack was taken; but we regret to say, that Joe has, for the present, escaped; the other corps are still in pursuit.

The spirit and alacrity evinced by the different military corps, in their laborious and indefatigable pursuit, entitle them to the highest commendation—their activity and zeal will, we trust, have a beneficial and lasting effect.

The Coroner's Jury, convened on the late melancholy occasion, have pronounced that the deceased came to his death by being "Murdered by three negroes unknown."

We understand that the two negroes now in custody, will have their trial tomorrow, at the court-house.

1. *Charleston Courier,* June 1, 1821; also printed in the *Charleston City Gazette,* June 1, 1821.

2. The records of the members of the Methodist church in Georgetown note that George R. Ford had joined on December 10, 1820, and "was murdered by Negroes May 26, 1821 but without doubt in heaven he rests from all trouble" (Georgetown Methodist Church records, South Carolina Historical Society). Ford was the owner of forty-five slaves on South Island, according to the 1820 census.

3. May 27, 1821; this is the day after the church records say Ford was killed but accords with document 5.12.

4. A crossing of the Congaree River more than a hundred miles upstream of Ford's plantation between Richland and Orangeburg districts.

5. May 31, 1821.

5.11] *Trial of Jack for the murder of George Ford*[1]

GEORGETOWN, JUNE 2.

A Court of Magistrates and Freeholders was convened on Thursday last, for the trial of *Jack,* the property of Mr. Fonqurg [sic][2] of Lancaster district, charged with the murder of George R. Ford, Esq. The Court consisted of the following persons:

John L. Wilson J. Q.
Henry L. Carnes J. Q.
Wm. W. Trapier
Francis Withers
Solomon Cohen
Robert Heriot
Aaron Marvin Freeholders

The evidence was very conclusive that he was either the actual perpetrator of the deed, or so far an accomplice, as to have been at the elbow of him that shot the fatal gun. The sentence of the law was therefore pronounced, *and will be executed on Friday next the 8th* inst. when he will be hung near this town. During the whole trial the prisoner exhibited no one mark of penitence or sorrow, but preserved the utmost stubbornness of features and of manner. The trial of the other fellow called Jack, the property of Mrs. Horry, has been postponed in order to have his testimony as to the identity of Joe, who is yet in the neighborhood of Lucas' plantation on Santee,[3] and who it is supposed will be taken. He threatens to sell his life dearly, and declares he will not be taken alive. Volunteer parties are still going out, to assist their fellow-citizens in the discharge of a very important duty.

No circumstance, within our recollection, has ever produced so great an excitement, in our community, as that occasioned by the late unprovoked and dreadful murder of our worthy fellow-citizen, GEORGE R. FORD, Esq. Amidst the painful feelings which it has produced, it is however consolatory to observe the universal sympathy which pervades the breasts of every class of the community—the exertions of the militia have been unremitted; from Monday last to the present moment, they have been day and night occupied in scouring the woods and swamps to the distance of twenty or thirty miles from town, notwithstanding the extreme heat of the weather and the heavy showers to which they have been exposed. It is with pleasure we notice the very prompt and satisfactory reply of His Excellency THOMAS BENNETT, to the communication made to him on this subject by the Intendant.

1. *Charleston Courier,* June 4, 1821.
2. This was a misspelling of Fonberg.
3. This plantation was a short way upstream, near the canal that connected the Santee River and Winyaw Bay.

5.12] *Rewards for the capture of Joe offered by the governor of South Carolina and by local residents*[1]

Proclamation.

By His Excellency THOMAS BENNETT,

Governor and Commander in Chief, in and over the State of So. Carolina.

Whereas certain evil disposed runaways have assembled on South-Island, in Georgetown District, where they have committed several daring depredations and on Sunday night the 27th May (instant,) committed a most daring and unprovoked Murder, by shooting George R. Ford, Esquire; and whereas public security requires the apprehension and punishment of these dangerous runaways; I deem it proper to issue this my Proclamation, and do hereby offer a reward of TWO HUNDRED DOLLARS for the apprehension and conviction of either of the following negroes, who are supposed to be the perpetrators of the aforesaid violence, viz; JACK, a short thick set, athletic man, black, projecting forehead, dark, heavy and lowering eyebrows, a terrible expression of countenance, about 5 feet 7 inches high; is a Virginian by birth, was brought to this State by a Mr. Sibley and is owned by a Mr. Fonberg of Lancaster district,[2] who lives about fifteen miles from the village.

JOE, is of an Indian complexion, has a scar on one of his cheeks, (believed to be the right) occasioned by the bite of a negro in a fight; a scar from the cut of a sabre, believed to be on his right arm; has shot marks in both of his legs, is in the prime of life, a very stout and athletic man, at least six feet high.

The late offence committed by them on South-Island, induced them to abandon their late camp in that neighborhood, and it was their intention on getting their clothes, to ascend the Santee, and take post at their old camp on the Wateree, in the swamp made by the confluence of Thomas's Creek and said River. The road they will take it is believed, will be on the South side of Santee, crossing the Canal at the Double Locks and crossing the Congaree at McCord's ferry. Joe has a wife at Mr. McCord's by the name of Dinah or Diannah, and is well acquainted with the negroes in that neighbourhood.

The Camp is on the bank of the Wateree, and so situated as to command (through the canes) a view of every passenger on the river. Joe'[s] owner is unknown.

Given under my hand and the seal of the State, at Charleston [torn] day of May, in the year of our [torn: Lord one thousand, eight hundred a]nd twenty one

His Excellency the Governor, has offered by Proclamation, a reward of Two Hundred Dollars, for the apprehension of Joe, and about $300 more have been already obtained for the same object, by subscription, among the Citizens of Georgetown and its vicinity.[3]

1. Proclamation of Gov. Thomas Bennett, South Carolina Historical Society.

2. The Catawba River in Lancaster District feeds the Wateree, which in turn forms the Santee. This was perhaps Jacob Funderburgh, listed as the owner of twelve slaves in Lancaster District in the 1820 census.

3. *Charleston City Gazette*, June 4, 1821.

5.13 *Henry Carnes claims the governor's reward*

George Town June 12th 1821

I certify that the fellow called Jack, one of the murderers of George R. Ford Esqr & for whose apprehension a reward of Two Hundred Dollars was offered by a proclamation of his Excellency Thomas Bennett, was brought in by a Detachment of the "Columbian Greens" under the command of their Captain Henry L. Carnes, who I have every reason to believe apprehended the said negro; nor do I know of any other person, or persons, laying any claim to the above reward: I further certify that the above mentioned negro Jack, was tried, & condemned for the said murder, and that he was executed on Friday last.

Robert Heriot

Intendant of the Town of George Town.

Received Charleston June 12, 1821 from Tho: Bennett Governor of the State of S⁰ Carolina Two Hundred Dollars being the amount of a reward offered by Proclamation for apprehending a fellow named Jack subsequently convicted of the murder of Mr. Ford

$200 H. L. Carnes.[1]

1. Governor's messages, 1822, 1301–53, South Carolina Archives.

5.14] *Claim of Meshack Williams*

The honorable the Speaker and other Members of the House of Representatives of the State of South Carolina[1]

The Petition of Mesheck Williams respectfully sheweth, That your Petitioner was the Keeper of the House and Ferry (known by the name of South Santee Ferry, in the Parish of St. James' Santee) at the time the two companies (on the North & South side of Santee River) were in search of the Fellow Joe, the Murderer of M[r] George Ford, and that his house was made by the Commanding Officers, the Rendesvous for several days and that agreeably to their Orders, the Subalterns & Privates were ferried to and fro and were furnished by the Petitioner with such supplies for themselves and Horses as were ordered by the Commanding Officer, for which, he has never received payment, he now presents his accounts properly vouched and respectfully prays that your Honorable body will take ~~the same~~ his claim into consideration and grant him the relief he is so justly entitled to, & he will as in duty bond every pray &c

St James Santee Novr 20: 1822   Mesheck Williams
Granted 168.62^{1/2}$

In the House of Representatives, December 4, 1822[2]

The committee on claims, to whom was referred the petition of Meshack Williams, praying compensation for supplies furnished the militia in the services of the state, beg leave respectively to *Report*, That they have had the petition and documents accompanying it under consideration, and find that during the spring of 1821, a party of negroes embodied near the plantation of Mrs. Horry,[3] on Santee, had assembled on South-Island shore: they murdered Mr. George Ford, a citizen of this state. The committee also find that detachments of militia were ordered on duty, with a view to the apprehending the said negroes, and that the petitioner furnished the said detachments with supplies while on duty, to the amount of one hundred and sixty-eight dollars sixty-two and a half cents, which your committee deem a moderate charge. They therefore respectfully recommend that they prayer of the petition be granted, and that the sum of one hundred and sixty-eight dollars sixty-two and a half cents be appropriated for that purpose.

Resolved, That the house do agree to the report. Ordered, That it be sent to the senate for concurrence.

By order of the House,   R. ANDERSON, C.H.R.

In the Senate, December 6, 1822.

Resolved, That senate do concur in the report. Ordered, That it be returned to the house of representatives.

By order of the Senate,   WM. D. MARTIN, C.S.

1. South Carolina General Assembly petitions, 1822, no. 46; verbatim copy to the Senate, 1822, no. 67.

2. Acts and resolutions of the General Assembly, 1822, General Assembly record series S165005, 1822, no. 65, South Carolina Archives.

3. The Horry plantation was near the canal connecting the Santee with Winyaw Bay.

5.15] *Newspapers continue to report on the hunt for Joe*

Two detachments of Militia from Georgetown, (S.C.) have been *rogue-hunting*, for several days, in search of Negro Joe, supposed to have been the murderer of Mr. Ford. They traced him to a Swamp, but were unable to find him. He is an artful and bold fellow, and approaches in hardihood to the character of "Three Fingered Jack," the celebrated bandit of Jamaica.[1]

A letter received in town, written yesterday at the 32 Mile House, states that the fellow JOE, who murdered Mr Ford, has not yet been apprehended; and that he had escaped from the North to the South side of the river. Capt. Shackelford's and Huggin's companies were still using all their vigilance for his detection. They were stationed on different sides of the river.[2]

GEORGETOWN, JUNE 9.

EXECUTION—*Jack,* one of the murderers of Mr. FORD, was agreeable to his sentence, hung yesterday, and his body given to the Surgeons for dissection. He was conducted from the gaol to the place of execution, under an escort composed of the Columbian Blues and the Washington Greens.

We regret to state that *Joe,* the villain implicated in the murder of Mr. Ford, has not yet been apprehended; it is nearly a fortnight since the pursuit was commenced, and it is still kept up with ardor. He has been several times driven into such situations as afforded the strongest hopes of his being taken; but the intelligence and support furnished him from some of the neighboring plantations have hitherto assisted him to elude his pursuers. He some days since attempted to ascend the Santee, but was so closely pressed that he was constrained to abandon his canoe, with his provisions and part of his clothing, and again betake himself to the deep recesses of the swamps and cane-breaks. We have the best reason to believe that he is still on the northern bank of North Santee, a few miles above the great mail road, at a place called the *Cove.* He has, for the present, concealed himself in a peninsula, or narrow strip of swamp, bounded by the Santee on one side, and a lake, which unites with the river, on the other. There is but one point at which he could escape by land, and that, we understand, is closely guarded.—We have been thus particular for the information of those of our public spirited fellow-citizens, in other parts of the state, who may be 'on the alert' to detect this murderer, in the event of his eluding his pursuers in this neighborhood.

On Wednesday last, he entered the house of a free man, and, after snapping his gun at the woman of the house, he obliged her to give him a considerable quantity of bacon, corn and ammunition, and from thence, with his booty, he entered the swamp, in which, it is believed, he is at present.

If we might be allowed to draw some consolation from the circumstance arising out of the dreadful deed perpetrated by this blood-thirsty villain and his accomplices, we would be gratified in believing that the vigilance and activity of our volunteer detachments have not been without their benefit; for we have learned from some of our respectable citizens, who have been engaged in this unpleasant though essential duty, that they never witnessed stronger evidences of long existing licentiousness and want of subordination than were apparent on some of the plantations visited by them. We make this statement with reluctance;

but we believe that by making it, we perform a duty we owe to the public, and with us this duty shall be ever paramount to every other consideration.³

GEORGETOWN JUNE 13

We have good reason for believing that *Joe*, one of the murderers of Mr. Ford, has escaped the vigilance of his pursuers in this neighbourhood—there are still several volunteers out, but there appears to be little doubt of his having eluded them, and that he is making the best of his way up the Santee to his former resort, or that he is endeavouring to cross the country to Pee Dee, and from thence to pass into the state of North-Carolina. We embrace this earliest opportunity of notifying our fellow citizens in the interior of this fact, confident that they will use every means in their power to apprehend this villain.⁴

JOE—We offer to our readers, the following interesting extract from a letter received last evening, from Capt. Wm. S. Harvey, who resides near the head waters of the Sampit, about 13 miles from Georgetown; from which it will be seen, that the daring villain, Joe, and some of his accomplices, are yet in this neighborhood. The amount offered for the apprehension of JOE, including the sum mentioned in the Proclamation of the President, is about five hundred and fifty dollars; and it is expected that it will be considerably increased, as a number of our citizens have not yet contributed.

"*June* 22—After a day of great fatigue, about six o'clock, P M. yesterday, I was attracted by a smoke on the side of a small branch, about half a mile from my plantation; I advanced within 300 yards of it, before I could see any thing—I then beheld the villain Joe, cooking; I then took advantage of the smoke, and approached to within 150 yards of him. My boy Joe (the only person with me) had started with the intention of getting in the rear of the branch. I was now compelled to wave him to return; by which means the fellow saw me, and made a wheel to the left about, took up his gun and fled to the branch, where I dare not follow him, he being covered and I exposed. Before I got my boy up to me, the murderer had gained on me, by keeping the middle of the branch. He could not have been more than 80 or 90 yards from me—judging from the cracking of the branch. Hearing he had with him, a stout black fellow, armed, I thought it advisable to retreat, fearing they would cut me off from my boat, in which I had crossed Gravely Gully.⁵ He is over 6 feet, and will weigh 200 lbs—he moved heavy but strides long—is not very yellow—his clothes brown—carries a large pack, through which no ball can well penetrate. If he is cowardly in the day, he is bold in the night. About 12 o'clock last night, I was awoke by the cattle in my lane, being harassed, not exceeding 20 yards from my door. I endeavoured to alarm my negroes; succeeded in getting one up, who, after examining, returned, saying the cattle were penned up in the lane but saw no one. I guarded them until near day-light. This was in the rear of my house. In front, on the paling, hung my large Seine, the lead line of which was cut, and about 6lbs of lead taken. I saw this morning, when I looked at the Seine, the tracks of three persons— they came from the side I saw Joe. After taking the lead, they went to my landing, and look my smallest canoe. I have three fellows in search of the canoe, and small flat, which is also missing. The flat, is but 15 feet long, and 8 wide, and can be taken any where by four able bodied men. I find myself very unwell, or I would be in search of these villains."[6]

Apprehension of Joe—We understand from a gentleman who arrived this morning from Santee, that the above fellow, who shot Mr Ford, of Georgetown, on the 27th ult. and for whom a reward of two hundred dollars was offered by the Governor, has been at last apprehended, and will not doubt soon atone for his crime by a public execution. We learn that he was seen lurking about Mr. White's plantation, at the upper part of St. James', Santee, on last Saturday night;[7] and that the superintendent (a young gentleman) being apprized of the fact, courageously marched out with a musket and secreted himself until JOE was within few yards of him. He then called on him to surrender and threatened instantly to take his life in case of refusal; Joe, who was also armed, but could not take an aim at his antagonist from the position he had taken, immediately retreated, when he was fired at and shot in the leg by his pursuer, at the distance of about forty steps.—*Patriot*

GEORGETOWN, JUNE 27.

JACK, who had been for several weeks confined in the jail in this town, on a charge of being an accomplice in the murder lately committed on South Island, was tried on Monday last: he was pronounced guilty by the Court, and sentenced to be hung, on Friday the 6th July, at Lockey's Bridge, between the Santee and Winyaw Bay.[8]

GEORGETOWN, JUNE 30

A report has been in circulation for day or two past, that the negro who shot Mr. Ford, had been wounded and apprehended near a Mr. White's plantation, in St. James,' Santee, but we fear that the report is unfounded. We have been unable to collect any information in corroboration of it, and the Southern mail carrier, who arrived here this morning, informs us that the volunteer detachment, which went down to take charge of the prisoner, is returning without him.

We have received a communication from Turkey Creek, in Williamsburgh district, stating that on Sunday morning last, two negroes entered the house of a gentleman of that neighborhood, during his absence. One of them our correspondent describes, as an elderly man of very black complexion; the other a stout mulatto; the latter was armed with a gun, and appeared to be well provided with ammunition; his companion addressed him by the name of Joe, and our correspondent thinks this is the fellow implicated in the murder committed on South-Island. They took from the house about two pounds of shot and some powder. A negro girl was the only person in the house when they entered, and on her observing that she would call her master, the fellow called Joe, swore that if he dared approach he would shoot him, and on the servant's attempting to leave the house, they seized her, and threatened her with instant death should she give any alarm. In a few minutes after their departure the owner of the house returned, and having alarmed the neighborhood, pursuit was commenced but without effect. The writer of this communication believes that it was their intention to cross the Black river at Kingstree, or at the lower bridge.[9]

The Charleston Times of July 2d, contradicts the report of the apprehension of Joe, the murderer of Mr. Ford. The subtle African continues his lodgement in the border of the swamps, and prowls around the neighbouring settlements, in defiance of all the efforts that have been made to apprehend him.[10]

GEORGETOWN, JULY 11

The negro Jack, who was some time since condemned and ordered to be executed, as an accomplice or associate with the negroes who murdered Mr. Ford, has been reprieved by his Excellency Governor Bennett.[11]

We are informed that the negro Jack, who was lately condemned at Georgetown, to be hung, as an accomplice or associate in the murder of Mr. Ford, has been pardoned by the Governor, pursuant to the unanimous recommendation of the court by whom he was tried, and on condition of perpetual banishment from the State.

The detachment of Washington Greens which left Georgetown on Tuesday for the purpose of examining the Negro lately taking in St. Thomas' Parish, supposed to be Joe, the murderer, have returned. The Negro proves to be the property of a Mr. Ashby, of that Parish, and not Joe.[12]

1. *Boston Commercial Gazette,* June 6, 1821. Three-Fingered Jack was a "Robin Hood" outlaw in Jamaica in 1780. As a maroon he successfully evaded white attempts to capture him, but, like Joe, other slaves were eventually responsible for his death. Jack's story spawned a literature of poems, ballads, and plays that celebrated his achievements. For one example, see William Earle, *Obi; or, The History of Three-Fingered Jack. In a Series of Letters from a Resident in Jamaica to His Friend in England* (London: Earle and Hemet, 1800).

2. *Savannah Georgian,* June 13, 1821.

3. *Charleston Courier,* June 11, 1821.

4. *Charleston Courier,* June 15, 1821.

5. This creek ran from south to north into Sampit Creek west of Georgetown.

6. *Charleston City Gazette,* June 25, 1821.

7. June 23, 1821. The White plantation was near Echau Church in St. James' Santee Parish, a few miles south of the Santee River.

8. *Charleston Courier,* June 29, 1821; also reported in the *Savannah Georgian,* July 3, 1821.

9. *Charleston Courier,* July 2, 1821; also reported in the *Savannah Georgian,* July 3, 1821. Kingstree is more than twenty miles north of the Santee River.

10. *Providence Gazette,* July 18, 1821.

11. *Charleston Courier,* July 13, 1821.

12. *Savannah Georgian,* July 19, 1821.

Two newspaper reports in November 1822 of a maroon gang attacking travelers on the main southwestern road out of Charleston are evidence that Joe was not the only fugitive slave striking back against white authority in South Carolina. This road was close to the swamps contiguous to the Stono River, which permitted maroons to disappear quickly after their attacks. As document 5.16 makes clear, not all victims were white. Gov. Thomas Bennett ordered the militia to attack the maroons, but with only limited success (document 5.17). In this letter he also makes reference to the hunt for Joe and his followers still at large on the Santee River.

5.16] *Reports of maroons attacking travelers outside Charleston*

Travellers Beware.—A gang of armed runaways are at present infesting the New-Bridge Road, in St. Andrew's Parish, and robbing passengers. On Wednesday last, several negroes were stopped and money and clothes taken from them and their persons kept in custody 'till after night. The clothes were of white plains with blue collars and cuffs to the coats. The robbers immediately dressed themselves in their spoil, which circumstance will probably lead to their discovery. Their range lies between the four and eight mile posts, and their depredations are committed in open day.—They sent insulting and menacing messages to the masters of those whom they had robbed, as to what they would do in case of their being pursued.—*Southern Patriot.*[1]

CHARLESTON, Nov, 11.

We understand that persons who are compelled to travel along the road over the New Bridge, are continually robbed by a gang of armed runaway Negroes, who, as we mentioned a few days past, are hovering about that place. Several depredations were committed on Saturday last by these fellows. Eleven of them were seen near the eight mile post, armed with muskets, cutlasses and hatchets. We trust that prompt measures will be adopted to put a stop to these shameful robberies.—*Patriot.*[2]

1. *Charleston City Gazette,* November 2, 1822.

2. *Baltimore Patriot,* November 19, 1822.

5.17] *The governor reports on militia action against the maroons*[1]

Executive Department
Columbia Decr 9, 1822
To the Senate of South Carolina
Fellow Citizens.

I hasten to comply with your request calling for information relative to the detachment of State Militia ordered out for the purpose of arresting several runaway slaves in the Parishes adjacent to Charleston.

It appeared from various communications made by respectable citizens of John's Island that a number of armed fugitive slaves were infesting that Parish, destroying the cattle, breaking into and robbing the dwellings, and threatening the lives of their most faithful domestics. On receiving this information I deemed it expedient to order Capt Jos. Jenkins who commanded that Beat to attempt their apprehension. The order was promptly obeyed, and with as much secrecy as the nature of the service permitted, Capt Jenkins arrived at their camp before their fires were extinguished and but a few moments after they had left it. This vigilant officer continued the pursuit for two days and nights and until he had received information that they had fled from his precinct. Col. Cattell minutely acquainted with the topography of St Andrew's where it was represented that they had renewed their depredations was requested to institute an inquiry into the facts and suggest a more successful mode of apprehending them. At much personal inconvenience, he (a very few days previous to his departure from Charleston to resume his legislative duties on the floor of the Senate), he kindly attempted a compliance with this request and after acquiring the requisite information, suggested the only expedient which promised certain success. In my official capacity the plan recommended could not be effected, and the alternative was to order out simultaneously the Beat companies of John's Island and St. Andrew's Parish. This order was issued four days before my departure from the city and executed since. It is therefore not possible (as no communication has reached me from the commanding officer of the detachment) to give with precision the information required. I would however respectfully recommend that a sum not exceeding Five Hundred Dollars ($500) be placed at the disposal of my successor for the purpose of defraying the expences of that detachment. The interests of the State will be thus protected and the amount expended in this service promptly returned.

Another detachment under the command of Capt. Huggins were in obedience to the militia Laws of this State engaged in a similar service. The daring and atrocious murderer of M^r. Ford of Georgetown had fled for concealment to the swamps of the Santee. This gentleman was not only actively engaged in the pursuit, but has been represented to have borne the whole expenses of that detachment which continued on duty without interference for a fortnight. This service was extremely arduous and attended with various privations and exposure at an inclement season. The expences of this detachment are represented to exceed five Hundred Dollars; no returns were made to this Department.

Those with the detachments adverted to in my second message comprehend all that have performed this service, within my knowledge.

Tho. Bennett

1. Governor's messages, 1822, no. 1325, South Carolina Archives.

Despite the efforts of militia units, Joe evaded capture. Rumors of his capture continued to appear in the newspapers, perhaps to reassure people that he would eventually pay for the murder of George Ford. By 1823 Joe had returned to his old camp at the confluence of the Wateree and the Congaree, where he continued to act as a magnet for new runaways and raid local plantations.

5.18] **Joe continues to evade capture**

The negro fellow Joe, the murderer of Mr Ford, near Georgetown, is said to have been discovered near his old ground on the Wateree in South Carolina. He was fired upon, and it is supposed mortally wounded.¹

The Murderer Joe—The following extract from a letter of a gentlemen of respectability, was put into our hands yesterday, by his correspondent. The writer states that he has been requested to inform the citizens in this neighbourhood "That Joe, the murderer of Mr. Ford, had gone back to his own range—Mrs. Horry's plantation. He was pursued in Clarendon a short time ago, and followed as far as Vance's ferry;² two of his companions were taken, who stated it was their intention to go to the plantation of Mrs. Horry. Joe is armed, and is quite lame from the wound he received when shot at over the river, of which you have no doubt heard."³

The Georgetown Intelligencer states, that the negro fellow who some time ago murdered Mr Ford in South Carolina, and who has thus long eluded justice, has been taken near Statesburg.⁴

Extract of a letter, dated
MANCHESTER, September 1, 1823
It will be recollected that three years since, Mr Ford of Georgetown, was cruelly murdered by a negro felloe (Joe) then fugitive, and belonging to Mr. Carrol,⁵ in the Fork. Immediately after the event had occurred, means were taken to secure him. To aid it the executive offered a reward of $—and the family

another of $—(it is believed) to bring him to punishment. All this was without any desirable result; for singular to say, the advertisement offering these rewards has been discontinued, while this accomplished villain has been pursuing his course of plunder in the most tranquil and uninterrupted manner.

The districts he has chosen for his residence and depredations have been the fork formed by the Wateree and Congaree and the eastern banks of the Wateree and Santee from Manchester to Nelson's Ferry.[6] He uses the most dense and impervious swamps, places himself at the head of fugitive slaves, arms them (their number is various and uncertain) and has continued a course of depredations which has terminated *for the present* in the murder of a valuable slave of Col. J. B. Richardson. He had long threatened this man's life in consequence of his having been the means of rescuing a negro woman of Dr. Raoul's whom he detained against her will for some months as his wife.—Aided by four others, *all well armed,* he entered Col. R's field on the 29th ult. about ten o'clock, A. M. and shot this negro amidst the others there at work. Col. R's overseer has also been the subject of his threats. On this occasion he directed his gun towards him repeatedly. Fortunately it missed fire; but the poor negro lingered till the 31st and then died.[7]

The negro fellow Joe, who about two or three years since, murdered Mr Ford of Georgetown, and eluded every attempt to take him, it has recently been discovered, has located himself in the fork formed by the Wateree and Congaree and the eastern banks of the Wateree and Santee rivers from Manchester to Nelson's Ferry (S.C.). He has here pursued uninterruptedly, his career of plunder since that period, and yet eludes all attempts to take him. He is accompanied by several other runaways. And has lately shot a valuable slave of Col J B Richardson,[8] who was instrumental in rescuing a negro woman whom he detained against her will as his wife.[9]

1. *Savannah Georgian,* October 9, 1821.
2. A crossing of the Santee between Sumter and Orangeburg districts.
3. *Charleston City Gazette,* November 22, 1822.
4. *Savannah Georgian,* April 19, 1823.
5. This is the first mention of Joe's owner. The Carroll family owned several tracts in Richland District on Tom's Creek, which ran southward into the Congaree swamps. See the will of Jacob Carroll, April 18, 1815, Richland County wills, box 4, item 99, South Carolina Archives. Although Jacob Carroll owned ten slaves at the time of his death, none of them was named Joe. It is possible that Joe was already a fugitive by 1815, but it is equally possible that he had been purchased by one of Carroll's five sons after 1815.
6. Both in Sumter District.
7. *Southern Chronicle,* September 17, 1823.
8. A creek on Richardson's plantation ran directly into the Santee.
9. *Savannah Georgian,* September 13, 1823.

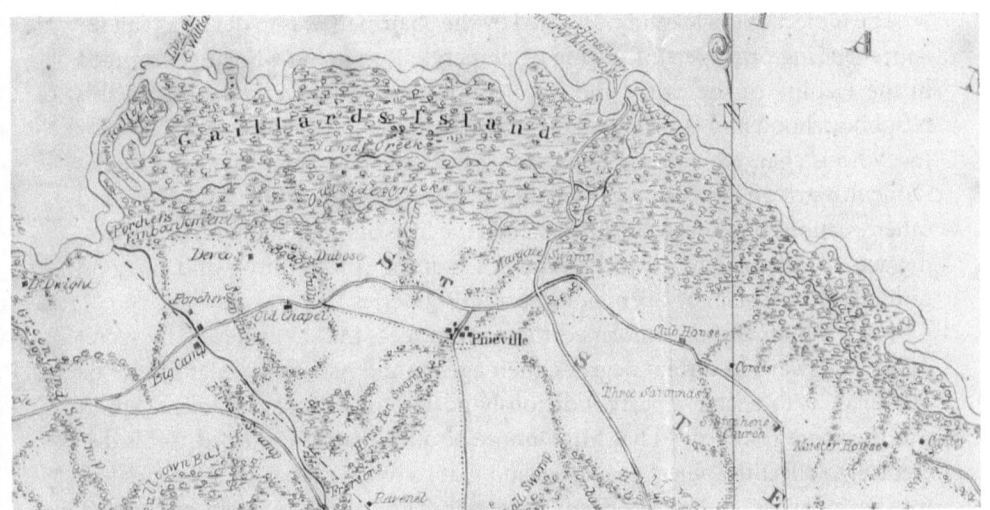

Charleston District, South Carolina, surveyed by Charles Vignoles and Henry Ravenel, 1820; improved for *Mills' Atlas*, 1825. Baltimore: Lucas, 1825. Courtesy of the Library of Congress, Geography and Map Division

The local residents of Pineville formed the Pineville Police Association[1] in October 1823 specifically to deal with the threat posed by Joe and his gang. The minutes of this association (document 5.19) tell us a good deal about the fears and concerns of white planters. The association adopted a tactic of divide and rule by offering inducements to slaves to help them. This reaped immediate dividends: within days Joe was dead, and over the ensuing days many of his gang were either captured or killed. Some maroons evidently managed to remain in the swamps since the Pineville Police Association was still pursuing them a year later. The journal of local planter Thomas Porcher (document 5.20) provides a personal record of the death of Joe. Further perspectives come from newspaper accounts of Joe's death (document 5.21).

1. For more on such associations, see Jack Kenny Williams, "Catching the Criminal in Nineteenth Century South Carolina," *Journal of Criminal Law, Criminology, and Police Science* 46 (July–August 1955): 264–71. In 1839 the constitution of the Pineville Police Association gave its purpose as "the enforcement of a rigid system of police & the suppression of all traffick with slaves."

5.19] Local residents organize to defeat Joe

Proceedings of the Standing-Committee.[1]
October 2nd 1823
Agreeably to Notice given the committee convened in the Library Room.

The Object of the Meeting, as stated by the chairman, was to devise a plan for apprehending or dispersing a gang of desperate Runaways, who are encamped in the vicinity of the canal, and have committed many Depredations in this Neighbourhood and elsewhere. One of the Number is a Fellow called Forest or Joe, who is charged with the murder of Mr. Ford. This Party, sheltered by the Difficulties of an approach to their camp and strengthened by Fire-Arms and other weapons of offence, have threatened the lives of many Individuals; by daring acts of villainy have disturbed the Peace of the community—and carry on unmolested a system of open violence and Robberies.

Mr. William Dubose informed the committee—that he believed, by secret offers of Reward to certain negroes, their agency and Assistance might so far be obtained, as to enable a party judiciously posted to surprise and take them. It was therefore resolved—That Mr. Dubose be authorised to proceed, at his discretion, to effect the object proposed; and that so much money be appropriated, for that purpose, as he may deem necessary. The committee then adjourned.

Thomas Gaillard Sec. & Treas

October 5th 1823—

The committee convened at Mexico[2] whither they had gone to meet a Party of Gentlemen who had on the preceding Day surprised and killed Joe and three of the Gang of Runaways.

Mr. Wm. Dubose communicated to the committee the measures he had adopted in pursuance of the Resolution of the 2n Inst—That by the active and ready co-operation of a fellow called Billy the property of Austin F. Peary a Plan had been devised; and but for Circumstances not within the controul of either Party complete success must have perfected their designs. This fellow had fulfilled with Fidelity the Duties imposed upon him, and had endangered his Life in the execution of them. He therefore presented to the committee his just claims for Remuneration.

On motion, it was resolved—That the Treasurer be directed immediately—to pay to the said Fellow Billy the sum of $20; and that an additional sum of $27 be paid to him on his return from Charleston. Also on motion resolved___That the chairman forthwith call upon the members of the Association for their support and aid in the Pursuit of the Remainder of the Gang who had not been taken.

The Committee then adjourned—
Thomas Gaillard
Sec & Treas

October 8th 1823

In consequence of the Apprehension of several of the Gang of Runaways who had been surprised in the Neighbourhood of the Canal, but had escaped and taken Refuge in the swamps below, a meeting of the committee was this day held in the Library Room.

On motion it was resolved that the President be instructed to proceed forthwith in the Name and in behalf of the Association, in the Prosecution of the said slaves, by having them brought before the proper Authorities; and that whatever expenses may be incurred in promoting the Objects of this Resolution, other than those payable by the State, shall be defrayed with the Funds of this Association.

Thomas Gaillard
Sec & Treas

August 5th 1824

At a meeting of the standing committee in the Library Room—it was resolved—That the Treasurer be instructed to pay to the constables—appointed to take out of the Gaol in Camden the Fellow (Isham) who had eluded the Pursuit of the Party last year—that he may be brought to his trial in this place—whatever expenses they may incur in executing the warrant for that purpose issued.

Thomas Gaillard
Sec & Treas

September 15th 1824

The standing committee convened by order of the President, in the Library Room—It was proposed and agreed to—that ten dollars ($50) be given to the Constables who were sent to Camden for Isham—in addition to what has been already given to them by the Resolution of the 5th Ins^{t}.—

Thomas Gaillard
Sec & Treas

1. Pineville Police Association, 1823–40, vol. 1; Secretary Book, South Carolina Historical Society. The only other mentions of fugitive slaves made in the records of this association, apart from those reproduced here, are in the accounts for 1827, which list payments of two dollars each to eight slaves for the capture of runaways.

2. Samuel Porcher's 1,516-acre plantation just east of the entrance to the Santee Canal on the Santee River. See *A Plan of Mexico Plantation* (1802), South Caroliniana Library, University of South Carolina, Columbia.

5.20] *Thomas Porcher's plantation journal*

Saturday October 4th [1823][1]

A party of men from P. V. went to endeavour to take Joe & his party last night but they did not succeed-

Sunday October 5th

There was a letter rec'd last night from Capt. Moor informing us that a party of 23 men had come down in their Canal Boats from the neighbourhood of Manchester & had killed Joe & three other negroes near their camp nearly opposite the Lock at the River—Most of the Gentlemen from here went up to White Oak[2] to see the Gentlemen—we had a better rain this evening.

1. Thomas Porcher plantation journal, 1822–23, South Carolina Historical Society. Thomas Porcher (1766–1835) was the owner of Ophir plantation, west of the Santee Canal, which is now submerged underneath Lake Moultrie.

2. White Oak plantation, at the entrance to the Santee Canal on the Santee River, was owned by Ralph Izard and was adjacent to Mexico plantation, owned by Samuel Porcher.

5.21] *Newspaper accounts of the death of Joe*

We have been informed by the Charleston Post rider that Col. Manning's Party have killed four of the negroes who have for some time past secreted themselves in fork of the Wateree and Congaree—and in the swamps on the Eastern side of the Santee and Wateree. Joe the murderer of Mr Ford is said to be of the number: his head was cut off and stuck on a pole at the mouth of the creek, as a solemn warning to vicious slaves. It is also stated that Col. Nixon's Isam was taken who is reputed to be very daring and desperate.[1]

The celebrated bandit Joe, the murderer of Mr Ford and Col. Richardson's driver, in South Carolina, has at last met his deserts. He was killed, with three of his gang, in his haunt by a party of gentlemen who went out for the purpose of taking him.[2]

From the Charleston Mercury
Pineville (S.C.) 5th Oct. 1823

Yesterday morning at an early hour, a party of gentlemen from Clarendon, who had been for several days in pursuit of the fellow called Forest or Joe, surprised the gang, of which this fellow appeared to be the leader, near the mouth of the Canal, and by a simultaneous attack effected the destruction of them all.

The progress of this fellow through different parts of the country was marked with the most daring outrages, and in open defiance of the laws. He invariably pointed out as objects of his vengeance every individual who manifested a disposition to check him in his career of violence, or to assist in his apprehension. He had a force, though very inconsiderable, completely under his direction; and being strengthened by the aid of fire arms, had under his control whatever boats navigated that section of the river. Indeed, by threats and persuasion, his communication through that means, with different parts of the country, had become very extensive; and his intimacy and influence over the negroes in the neighbourhood of his encampment, rendered every attempt which had been made to take him, abortive. The various channels through which he received information of every movement made or plan devised, to effect that object, enabled him to act with impunity in many instance, under circumstances and in places, which the most daring villainy would scarcely have conceived.[3]

More Negroes Destroyed
Extract of a letter, dated Pineville, Oct 13.
"A party went out on Tuesday last,[4] and routed the remainder of Joe's gang. They fired on two of the men and wounded one. One of the Negroes wounded Evance Cordes in the shoulder and one finger, with duck shot. The wound is very slight, and he is entirely recovered. On Wednesday, some of the same party went out, and came up with two men and three women. One of the men fired on John Ravenal, but without effect, and made his escape. They took one fellow and the wenches, and we have them now in confinement in this place. One of the women having a man's cloak on was fired upon, and I am sorry to say was wounded—her chance of recovery is doubtful.

"On Tuesday when the party were routed, they left a child about three years old in the camp, and a chance shot struck it in the back of the head, and it has since died. The fellow taken and the woman wounded, (who is the wife of Joe) belongs to Dr Raoul: a Girl, the mistress of Joe, belongs to Mr Ballard: and the other woman, the wife of Anderson who was killed, belongs to Mr Bates. Two of the most desperate and one woman, are not yet taken.

A Court of Magistrates was sitting for the trial of those taken, and others suspected. An Acting Committee of the Association are very active in gaining information."[5]

Extract of a letter, dated
Santee Canal, October 20th, 1823,—I am happy to inform you that all of the Company's Negroes are discharged, and declared innocent. Two of them only received a moderate correction, which however was not for being found guilty of having any connexion with those runaway negroes, but merely for their inconsistency in their evidence. One of Joe's gang name Stephon, belonging to Dr. Raoul, was hung close by the Canal Bridge,[6] on Friday last: and I hope that this unpleasant affair may be finally suppressed now.[7]

    1. *Southern Chronicle,* October 8, 1823. The last sentence of this report is contradicted by document 5.19, which makes it clear that Isam was not captured for another year.
    2. *Savannah Georgian,* October 11, 1823.
    3. *Milledgeville Recorder,* October 21, 1823.
    4. October 7, 1823.

5. *Southern Chronicle*, October 22, 1823.
6. A few miles west of Pineville in Charleston District.
7. *Southern Chronicle*, October 29, 1823.

As with other instances of attacks on maroon bands, the legislature received petitions for redress in the aftermath. Jean Lewis Raoul (document 5.22) unsuccessfully sought compensation for a slave executed as a member of Joe's gang. In document 5.23 local residents commend the behavior of Royal, who was instrumental in the final defeat of Joe. Document 5.24 makes it clear that Royal was not the only African American to assist whites against Joe.

5.22] Petition of Jean Lewis Raoul

State of South Carolina,[1]

To the honorable the president and the Speaker and the other members of the House of Representatives of the State of South Carolina

The humble petition of Jean Lewis Raoul Sheweth unto your honorable body, that about the month of September last, your petitioner was possessed of a negro man slave, named Stephon who had absconded from your petitioner and had joined a set of outlaws; that about the same time, the said negro man was apprehended, tried & convicted of divers felonies, of which he had been guilty, whilst he had so absconded as aforesaid from your petitioner & was executed.

And your petitioner further sheweth that he was also possessed of a negro woman who had been forced from the Employment of your petitioner by the famous out Law Joe, otherwise called Forest: which said woman was in the camp of these out Laws, when attacked that in firing into the camp, the said Negro woman was so severely wounded as to render her of no value, but on the other hand of Considerable Expense to your petitioner.

Whereupon your petitioner prays your honorable body to grant him a Compensation for the Said Slaves and your petitioner will every pray.

Raoul
South Carolina

I hereby certify that a certain Negro man slave named Stephon, the property of Dr. Raoul, was on ___ day of October last sentenced by a court of magistrates and freeholders to be hung on the Seventeenth day of October Last; which Sentence was put in execution in St. Stephens, Charleston District. Given under my hand & seal at Columbia, the fifth day of December A.D. One thousand eight hundred & twenty three

Sign'd P. S. Porcher.[2]

The committee on claims to whom was referred the Petition of Lewis Raoul praying compensation for a Negro executed & other purposes beg leave to report.[3]

That they have carefully Examined the same from which it appears that the Petitioner had a Negro Slave named Stephon that had run off and joined a party of out laws. That some time this last summer this fellow was apprehended, tried & executed being found guilty of various misdemeanors against [torn] of this state. Your petitioner, also [torn] negro woman, who was in the camp with those outlaws. And was wounded by being fired on in attempting their escape, which has rendered her of little or no use ever since. Your committee are of opinion that this fellow was in a state of open rebellion against the laws &c of this State and therefore not a case that is provided for under act of the Legislature in such cases made & provided. And would also remark that there were no certificate of court by which said slave was tried, as relates to the woman your committee are of opinion that inasmuch as she was wounded in the camp with those outlaws, it was certainly his misfortune, but are of opinion the petitioners have no just claims on the state. And would therefore respectfully recommend that the prayer of the Petition be not granted.

John K. Griffin
Chairman

1. South Carolina General Assembly petitions, 1823, no. 142. An identical petition to the Senate can be found in General Assembly petitions, 1823, no. 174.

2. A note on the back reads "rejected as in rebellion."

3. This report was accepted by the Senate on December 16, 1823 (South Carolina Legislative Records, S165005, 1823, 236).

5.23] *Petition to free Royal*

To the honorable, the president, and the senate of the legislature of the state of South Carolina[1]

We the subscribed Petitioners, inhabitants of Claremont, Clarendon, St. Johns, St. Stevens, and Richland Districts[2] beg leave to offer to your honorable and enlightened Body the following narrative as containing the grounds of their most reasonable petition. It is now some years since Mr. Ford a worthy and respectable Citizen of our state was murdered some where not far from Georgetown S°. Ca by a Negroe belonging to Mr. Carroll of Richland District named Joe (Or Forest). We believe that unhappy occurrence happened under the Executive administration of the honourable Thomas Bennett. The Relatives of Mr. Ford offered liberal rewards for the apprehension of this out lawed fellow. The Executive offered an appropriate reward also, but neither the temptation of the private reward, nor the public reward of the Governor, nor both combined could lead to his capture. He was so cunning and artful as to elude pursuit and so daring and bold at particular times when no force was at hand as to put everything at defiance. Emboldened by his successes and his seeming good fortune he plunged deeper and deeper into crime, until neither fear nor danger could deter him first from threatening and then from executing a train of mischiefs we believe quite without a parallel in this country.

Most of the runaways flew to his camp and he soon became their head and their life. He had the art and the address to inspire his followers with the most wild and dangerous enthusiasm. Such was his cunning that but few of the enterprises for mischief planned by himself fail'd of success. We believe that nearly four years have now elapsed since the murder of Mr. Ford, the whole of which time, until his merited death was marked by crimes, by mischiefs and by the desemination of notions the most dangerous among the blacks in ~~of~~ our sections of the country. (Such as were calculated in the end to produce insubordination and insurrections with all the hideous train of evils that usually follow. Such at length began as we believed to be the danger arising from the power and influence of this example and such we believed were the indications given of approaching insurrection, that we deemed it ~~propper~~ expedient to call on the propper military department to send an adequate force either to capture or destroy a species of enemy that kept our families and neighbourhoods in a constant state of uneasiness and alarm. This propper and justifiable application for assistance being disregarded; we made direct application to the commander-in-chief who taking no notice of our appeal to him we were compelled as we conceived from the necessity of the case to associate together for the purposes of domestic safety and for the object of impressing our blacks with propper fear by the power of wholesome example.

We cannot but think that the state authorities as well civil as military were bound not only to have aided and assisted in carying into effect these most laudable views but that they were bound also without delay to have attended to the peace and protection of an important and interesting section of the State of South Carolina for it is held as a just and fundamental maxim of government that States are bound to give to their citizens as adequate protection as possible in cases of alarm and danger. We organised several companies as Infantry, from among our association and being prepared for some days active service under persons chosen to command. We or many of us scoured Santee River Swamp from the confluence of the two rivers that form it to Murry's Ferry[3] a distance even by land of sixty miles. Notwithstanding however the zeal and alacrity with which we continued pursuit we should at length oppressed by the sultry sun of ~~August~~ October 1823 wearied down by excessive fatigue and rendered dispirited by the number extent and character of their places of retreat and concealment

~~should~~ have abandoned ~~their~~ our enterprise as being likely to yield nothing but disappointment to ourselves and triumph to the objects of our pursuit, but for the fidelity of a slave belonging to *Mrs. Perrin*[4] of Richland District *named Royal.* He in perfect good faith conducted a select party of your petitioners to the camp of Joe and his followers, and having the command of a boat, being its patroon, he with considerable judgement and address managed to decoy those whom we had long sought towards the boat, where were stationed a party expressly detailed for this duty. Soon perceiving their mistake and the danger full before them, they instantly attempted to defend themselves with well charged musquets but at a single well directed fire from the party of whites in the boat Joe with three of his party fell dead. The rest of the gang of runaways were subsequently either killed in pursuit, hung for attempts to murder or were frightened to their respective homes. Now therefore we your most humble and respectful petitioners conceiving that we particularly and that the state generally are deeply indebted to this slave Royal for his fidelity and good conduct in making himself the immediate instrument in bringing to merited punishment an offender, against the laws of the land, ~~and against the laws of God, of the worst character and of the highest gravity,~~ & pray that in due consideration of these things will award to him such compensation as may be fully adequate and as your honorable and enlighten'd body may think most compatible with the best interest of the state and with its dignity and character in rewarding those that have rendered services to it. The good faith and honor of your petitioners are implicated so far towards this slave on account of his good conduct and faithfulness that they are bound most earnestly to pray your honorable body to grant their prayer in which event they shall as in duty bound ever pray

John Mayrant Jr; Rich[d] Moore; Warner Mason; John China Jr; Isaac Norton; W. L. Brunson; Richard R. Spann; Isaac Linoir; Peter F. Welson; W. A. Caldon Jr; James Atkinson; H Vaughan: John A. Bowrider; Ja[s] S Spann; Wm. H. James; Hezekiah Nettles; Thos P. Evans; John Carter;

William D. Wilder A. P. Johnston; James H. Hext; T. N. Johnston; L. M. Brunson; Tho[s]. R. Morgan; John N. Carpenter; James B. Richardson; Jn[o] R. Spann; William Cad; W. H. B. Richardson; Charles Richardson; Isaac Porcher; H. Ravenel; David Gaillard; James Gaillard; Joseph Palmer; Robt. M. Cahusac; John S. Ravenel;

Wm. Sumter; Sam[l] E. Nelson; Sam[l] J. Murray; J. W. Mayrant; Robert M Compton; John J. Frierson; W. H. Capers; W[m]. R. Linoir; Martin Byrd; John Hudnall; W. Falconer; Peter J. Wright; Jn[o] R. Singleton; John Boyd Jun[r]; John James; A. B. Drake; David F. Nyles; A. C. Garz; James Libby;

Daniel Cahusac; W[m] Cain; Julius McKelvey; John G. R. Gardidier; R. W. McKelvey; R. M. Gourdin; Ransom D. McKelvey; Emanuel Levy; Edwin Gaillard;

Samuel Porcher; Theodore S. Gaillard; Dr. J. Ravenel; W. Dubose; Samuel Dubose; Thomas Gaillard; S. Legueiux; Stephen Deveaux; Charles Stevens; Thomas Porcher; Charles Porcher; Richard White; Wm. R. Right; John Couturier; Matt^w James

The committee on claims to whom was referred the petition of Sundry inhabitants of Clarendon, Claremont St James St Stephens and Richland Districts praying that a reward be given to the slave who led to the detection of the out law Joe beg leave to report.[5]

That they have duly considered the same, from which it appears that this Negro Joe was a fellow, who from the circumstances of his having murdered Mr Ford, with some others perhaps blacks, together with a series of villainy heretofore unparalleled in this state, had become a terror to a number of the petitioners with others. For the murder of Mr Ford there was a reward of a thousand dollars for his apprehension, and notwithstanding great exertions were made by the citizens in that quarter of the state for a considerable length of time to take the said fellow generally yet their efforts proved unavailing and had it not been for the interference and honest disclosure and management of a Negro fellow belonging to Mrs Perrin of Richland District by the name of Royal it is intirely uncertain to what extent the mischief and villainy of this fellow might not have grown. Under those circumstances and believing it to be the policy of this state to reward those slaves who thus distinguish themselves by way of inducement to others to do so likewise, your committee would therefore recommend that Co^l Edward Richardson be requested to wait on Mrs Perrin and ascertain whether she will part with the said Negro Royal and if so what she will be willing to take for him & that Mr Richardson be requested to report to the legislature at its next session.

John K Griffin. Chairman

December 11, 1824

The committee on claims to whom was referred a resolution directing that enquiry be made as to the propriety of rewarding the slave who gave the information which led to the detection of the outlaw Joe beg leave to report.[6]

That they have duly considered the same, and from the information which your committee have been able to obtain, it appears that this outlaw Joe was a fellow, who from the circumstances of his having murdered Mr Ford, with some others together with a series of villainy heretofore unparalleled in this state, had become a terror to the inhabitants in that part of the state.

For the murder of Mr Ford there was a reward of a thousand dollars offered for the apprehension of this fellow Joe, and notwithstanding great exertions were made by the citizens generally yet their efforts proved unavailing and had it not been for the interference Honest disclosures and good management of this fellow (by the name of) Royal (who it appears belongs to Mrs Perrin of Richland District) it is entirely uncertain to what extent the mischief and villainy of this fellow might not have gone.

Under those circumstances and believing it to be the policy of this state to reward those slaves who thus distinguish themselves by way of inducement to others to do so likewise, your committee would therefore recommend that the sum of seven hundred dollars be appropriated and paid to Mrs Perrin so soon as she does manumit her slave Royal on condition that she does manumit the said slave Royal in the course of three years from the present date.[7]

John K. Griffin chairman

Decr 14th 1825.

In Senate 16 Dec. 1825

Resolved that this House do agree to the Report. Ordered that it be sent to the House of Representatives.

In the House of Representatives. Dec. 17th 1825 Resolved that the House do agree to the Report. Ordered that it be returned.

1. South Carolina General Assembly, petition ND, no. 1874.

2. All of these districts bordered the Santee River. Claremont and Clarendon later formed part of Sumter County.

3. Williamsburg District.

4. Most likely the wife of Christian Perrin, the only Perrin in Richland District in the 1820 census. In 1820 the family owned sixteen slaves.

5. South Carolina General Assembly, committee reports, 1824, no. 270.

6. General Assembly, committee reports, 1825, no. 252. A verbatim copy was published in *Acts and Resolutions of the General Assembly of the State of South Carolina, Passed in December, 1825* (Columbia, S.C.: D and J. M. Faust, 1826), 102.

7. A detailed search of the state treasurer's records from this period failed to find any such payment made to Mrs. Perrin.

5.24] *Petition to reward Jack and Tom* [1]

To the Honorable the Speaker, and other members of the House of Representatives—

The undersigned citizens of Georgetown district, respectfully present to your honorable Body, that from the facts that have come to their knowledge in relation to the conduct of Jack, & Tom, and as a matter of public policy, they would pray that your Honorable Body would pay to the owners of the said slaves (for their use) a suitable & proper reward.

J. D. Coachman Clerk of Council

W. Dozier, Intendant

Henry L. Shaw

Stephen Farrow
Wm Dewson
M. C. Myas Members of the Town Council of Georgetown
State of South Carolina
Georgetown District

Personally appeared Eleazer Waterman, who being sworn says that during the year Eighteen Hundred & Twenty-Two the neighbourhood of Georgetown was infested by a gang of lawless & desperate runaways that in June said year George R. Ford Esquire was murdered on his own plantation by a part of this gang—that Jack & Tom (two negro men) at every hazard arrested one of the runaways, and it was through their means that the murderer was taken, brought to trial, and executed and the whole gang thus dispersed.

Eleazer Waterman owner of the negro Tom and Trustee of Elizabeth Shaw the present owner of Jack.

Sworn to before me this 22^d Nov 1834. James Smith[2]

1. South Carolina General Assembly petitions, 1834, no. 18.

2. A note on the back reads "Favourable $50 each." This petition was read in the Senate, December 5, 1834, and referred to the Committee on Claims. Its report was read in the Senate, December 9, 1834, recommending "that the sum of One hundred Dollars be paid to E. Waterman or his lawful attorney to be appropriated solely to the benefit of negroes Jack and Tom and to be equally divided between said Negroes," agreed by the Senate, December 17, 1834. See South Carolina Senate journal, 1834, South Carolina Archives.

The death of Joe and the scattering of his band of followers did not mark the end of marronage in this part of South Carolina. In 1824 and 1826 well-organized maroon camps were discovered near Georgetown, close to several large plantations, and despite assaults by local whites most of the maroons escaped (document 5.25).

5.25] *Newspaper reports of maroon communities near Georgetown in 1824 and 1826*

Georgetown (S.C.) Dec. 21[1]

On Friday evening a few gentlemen, headed by Col. Huggins, went down the bay in pursuit of a gang of runaway negroes, who were reported to be committing depredations in this neighbourhood. As the wind blow with great violence, they were obliged to stop that day at Mr. Fraser's plantation.[2] On Saturday four other gentlemen followed and joined the first party. They divided into three boats, succeeded in burning two large camps and some distance from each other, took two guns, some fishing apparatus, and other articles which had been in possession of the gang, and after a long chase, secured one of their number, a fellow by the name of Newton, the property of Mr. R. N. Magill.

The *three camps which have been destroyed, consisted of snug little habitations, and could have accommodated twenty men. At each of them there was a well. At one they had left chaff and straw enough to show that they must lately have pounded out at least fifty bushels of rice; at another place, there was a good stack yard and threshing place. The relics of ducks, turkeys, vegetables, and beef, which were found, proved that they had been abundantly provided with delicacies as well as necessaries. At one of the camps Mr. Fraser found some fine cabbages which had been recently cut from his garden. After cutting the cabbages, that no mistake might arise, they *crossed* each stock with a knife.

It appears from the information which has been received from Newton, and one or two negroes, who have been examined on suspicion of holding communion with them, that they have carried on an extensive traffic in the town, sometimes thro agents and occasionally themselves. These boats have usually landed *at the fort,* and they often amused themselves with promenades through the streets, unmolested by police or patroles.

The places of retreat were selected with great judgement. They are situated on small elevations, surrounded by extensive arrears of marsh. By climbing a high tree on each of them, a complete view of the bay, creeks and surrounding island, was presented to the spectator, while he could remain concealed by the foliage. No correct account of the number of the gang can be obtained. Reports are various and contradictory. That they have been continually aided and hold constant communication with many of the negroes of this town, there is conclusive evidence. Their leader is Will, the brother of Newton. He has sent a message to Mr. Thompson and Mr. Fraser, that if he ever should meet them, he will kill them. The witness states that he has twice taken deliberate aim at Mr. Thompson while passing through the woods on horse back, but fortunately his musket snapped. Proper measures have been taken to cut off his retreat; and as the pursuit still continues, it is probably that the whole band will within a day or two be secured. Had there not been great remissness in the execution of the patrole laws, they could not have escaped so long. *Gazette**

On Saturday last a party of gentlemen, 15 in number, and several trusty negroes, at the request of Capt. Vereen, met at Dr. Allston's Branch, on Pee Dee, to hunt a gang of runaway negroes, who were infesting the neighboring Plantations. After hunting very assiduously for several hours, they discovered a Camp in Gadsden Bay,[3] and started several negroes, but from the impenetrable nature of the swamp, it was impossible to overtake them—two guns were fired, but the gentlemen did not wish to hit the negroes. A large quantity of beef was found in the Camp, drying on scaffolds, four hides, a fine fat cow, supposed to belong

*One mentioned in a communication in the last gazette.

to Col. Hunt, hamstrung, pots, clothes, a hog pen, wells dug, and every necessary preparation for a long residence.

We hope the Black River gentlemen will attack the other side of the Bay, and by such means the negroes will become so uneasy they will probably go in to their owners.[4]

    1. *Charleston Mercury,* December 24, 1824.
    2. This plantation was on a headland on the eastern shore of Winyaw Bay.
    3. The Allston family owned several plantations on the Pee Dee River. The term "bay" was given to low-lying swampy areas between the rivers. It has not been possible to identify the precise location of Gadsden Bay; it is not marked on the detailed *Mills' Atlas* of 1825.
    4. *Georgetown Gazette,* June 13, 1826.

It was not just in the Santee River swamps that maroons found ready refuge during the 1820s. In 1823 the Savannah Georgian *reported that "A correspondent in Purysburg informs us, that a number of armed negroes were encamped in that neighborhood, and that several gentlemen had gone in pursuit of them."[1] This was precisely the same location that had supported large maroon bands in the eighteenth century (see chapters 2 and 3). In 1829 planters in Christ Church Parish, just north of Charleston, presented the legislature with a lengthy complaint (document 5.26) about the impact that maroons were having in their neighborhood. In particular they blamed an 1821 law, which set out new penalties for murdering slaves, for reducing the willingness of residents to hunt down runaways. This law had, they thought, fundamentally changed the heart of the relationship between masters and slaves and increasingly emboldened enslaved people to run away. Successful runaways were in turn an encouragement to others to follow suit. The anecdotal information given about the number and size of runaway groups gives us rare insight about the composition of maroon communities. A newspaper report (document 5.27) confirms that maroons were a particular problem in Christ Church Parish in 1829.*

    1. *Savannah Georgian,* March 13, 1823.

5.26] *Planters in Christ Church Parish summarize the problems with maroons*[1]

To the Honorable The President and Members of the Senate of South Carolina The Memorial of the Freeholders and other Inhabitants of the Parish of Christ Church Respectfully Sheweth

That Your Memorialists Planters of South Carolina, from the vicinity of their property to Charleston, from this Parish being surrounded by Navigable water leading directly to, and occasioning much intercourse with that city, and from the great Northern road passing through their parish in its whole length, are peculiarly exposed to the great evil of absconding slaves and their ruinous depredations.

Your Memorialists are aware that these causes have long combined to produce this evil, but they have in these latter years only, found it operate to an extent producing great irregularity and disorder among their slaves, and now leading directly to a state of insubordination and danger affecting the lives of individuals and the security of property.

This state of things is operating, your memorialists believe, in every part of the lower and middle divisions of the state, as they are informed by the Inhabitants of other parishes and it cries aloud for the interference of your Honorable Body.

They think it unnecessary to say any thing of the increasing efforts made by enthusiasts out of Carolina to poison the minds of our domestic people, these must be met in a different way, and cannot hurt us if the Southern States are true to themselves;[2] but they would distinctly state their conviction that great mischief has been already done, and is daily increasing by the misguided zeal and unguarded movements, acts and conversations of persons within our own state, owning little or none of the property they so earnestly and increasingly crave to meddle with, yet living and supported by the agriculture of the country.

Prior to the passing of the law of 1821[3] entitled an act to increase the punishment inflicted on persons convicted of murdering any slave and *for other purposes therein mentioned*,* it is asserted by your memorialists without fear of contradiction, the slaves of this part of South Carolina were in every respect more obedient and better servants, and infinitely more trust-worthy and faithful than they have been subsequently. Since the passing of that law—changes in the prices of our crops and consequently in the fortunes of many of our fellow citizens have taken place, and these changes have carried to Charleston for sale, large bodies of Negroes. The unrestrained intercourse of these with free blacks and low and worthless white people, during their sojourn there has infused in to the minds of the negroes ideas of emancipation and of insubordination, which they carry with them when sold into every part of the state.

Your memorialists have referred to the law of 1821, as a period from which the evils of running away have increased upon them and upon the low country, and they do not hesitate to say, that this law has produced a most baneful influence on the conduct of the negroes. The persons who projected that law stated no doubt that they were actuated by notions of great humanity but your memorialists with much deference to your Honorable Body undertake to assert that they were not practical Southern planters, otherwise they would have foreseen

---

* No other purposes are mentioned in this act!

that the law would be useless and even hurtful to those it professes to protect; these persons were not Southern legislators, for if they had been, they would have known that *changing the nature of the penalties in the case of negroes*—that inflicting the punishment of death on a white man for killing a slave, *who is a property, instead of exacting a fine for the loss of that property,* was placing the white inhabitants on a footing which would not be admitted by juries of our countrymen, and hence that the penalty never would be inflicted in any case however enormous; for the very effect of the law, as your Memorialists will presently show, is to produce upon the part of the Negro, such acts of violence as call immediate vengeance down upon them. Your memorialists therefore deny most unequivocally the policy, much less the necessity, of such a law as that of 1821, unless to satisfy the morbid feelings of those who wish to interfere with our slaves; and they further assert that the negroes of South Carolina were better protected by the laws and penalties which were founded by our forefathers, on the dictates of common sense and the nature of the property, than by the law of 1821, for the old laws, were practical, reasonable, and therefore carried into execution, while the new law which inflicts death without benefit of clergy on a white for Killing a slave, apparently admits of no mitigation or exception even if the slave should have ravished his daughter, attempted to kill himself, or burnt his dwelling, and is therefore only productive of injury to the slave, to his owner, and to the country.

Your Memorialists will now proceed to show in their own case, the real and practical effect of the law of 1821, and your Honorable Body will not be surprised at the consequences, when the concise and artful manner in which the law has been drawn up is considered, its peculiar fitness to impress upon the minds of slaves (to whom it is too often read) that they are now on a different footing as regards their owners and the whites, from what they formerly were; a footing approaching nearer to a state of emancipation from their authority, and of course to a state of unrestrained liberty and licentiousness.

And first—This law prevents planters and overseers from turning out to put down even large gangs of runaways, unless under very aggravating circumstances; because they will not subject themselves to be tried for their lives by City juries having notions and prejudices as to the propriety, and of course as to the very principle of the law itself, different from what every planter and owner of country property must have, nor will they expose themselves to endure the expense, vexation and loss of time, to which they may be and in some instances have been made liable under the law, although in the end honorably acquitted

Secondly—The Negroes finding a backwardness on the part of their owners and their neighbours to turn out, are encouraged to run off without cause or with a view to commit depredations. Finding these are not closely pursued, others are encouraged to follow the same course and those at home become disorderly and insubordinate. It is well known to your Honorable Body, *that a state of security in crime like this described*, must lead to greater and yet greater atrocities, hence the depredations upon our property, crops and cattle, have been enormous.

Thirdly—Such Negroes as have in consequence of this combination of fatal circumstances, *remained out for years* at length cease to respect the whites, become reckless of consequences, and choosing their opportunities during the sickly season of the year or when individuals are alone and supposed to be defenceless, attack them with a view to destroy them.

Fourthly—The end of this chain of consequences proceeding from a most injudicious and fatal law, the act of 1821, is death to the misguided slave and destruction to the property of your Memorialists, as will appear from the following facts supported upon the evidence of affidavits.

In 1822, a Negro belonging to the Estate of Spring, but formerly the property of a Parishioner deceased, absconded and came into the Parish as a runaway. In 1824, a fellow belonging to Mrs Legare joined him as a runaway was shot and killed in his company.

In 1825 a family five in number purchased at the sale of A. Vanderhorst, absconded and joined the same ring leader. They continued out until October last, when the children surrendered (one having been born in the woods) the father and mother both having been shot and killed.

In 1827 three negroes belonging to a Parishioner's estate returned in like manner after the sale of his effects, as runaways. One of them in January last snapped a gun heavily loaded with slugs at one of your Memorialists, who met him in the woods and who immediately shot the Negro. Another of these three Negroes in October last attacked another of your Memorialists with a knife fifteen inches long, stabbed him in the hand and would have cut his throat, but for assistance rendered in time to save him. In 1828 runaway slaves were collected from various parts of the parish, one was killed upon the spot and another severely wounded for the second time and taken.

In January last eighteen slaves the property of one of your Memorialists went off under their driver, and of these one fellow has been shot and killed, while the house of the owner has been pillaged by his own slaves, ten of whom are still out in a Neighbouring parish. The death of these Negroes has been brought on them by the aggravating circumstances attending their depredations, which were no longer to be tolerated or borne with, One Negro taken some months ago declared on his trial, that he had in three weeks destroyed forty head of cattle, and many of your Memorialists are altogether prevented from keeping stock of any kind, from these causes, after having large gangs of cattle, sheep and hogs entirely destroyed.

Your Memorialists could swell this statement with many circumstances at once ruinous to them, as well as most vexatious in their nature, for many of their slaves, although not killed by Gunshot have been transported or have died in the woods, and of diseases occasioned by running away. But they will not wear out the patience of Your Honorable Body, they would now rather, briefly, but with the utmost earnestness appeal for redress from so grievous a state of anarchy, occasioned by a spirit of infatuation which is abroad in our country touching our Negroes, they would in truth and sincerity, and in the name of humanity to their slaves, call for a repeal of a law (the act of 1821) which lays the foundation for such waste of Blood & property, and for a reestablishment of the Old State laws formerly in force. They would ask as a Means of undeceiving their misguided people, as a means of enabling Your Memorialists and all planters throughout the State, to bring their own and all other Negroes into that state of subjection and perfect control, without which they speedily bring destruction on themselves and ruin on their owners; they would ask of this Honorable Body, to pass an act declaring every slave who shall hereafter abscond, runaway or who may now be absent, Outlaws, deprived of the benefit of the laws, and out of the protection of the State, after the lapse of thirty days from his work without his owners permission.

And your Memorialists as in duty bound will ever pray.

John Jonah Murrell; Henry English; Elisha Whilden; George W. D. Scott; Frederick Steding; James Gregorie; Joseph Maybank; J. Hibbber; D. Jervey; A. V. Toomer; Paul Weston; John White; Elias Whilden Junr; John Naubin; John D. Murphey; J. Ladson Gregorie; J. H. H. Gregorie; Thomas Joy; R. J. Morrison; Daniel Legare; James R. Dean; Chas. C. Miller; John Jones.

1. South Carolina General Assembly petitions, 1829, no. 090. This memorial was read in the House of Representatives on December 9, 1829, and was referred to the Judiciary Committee, but no action was taken. See South Carolina House of Representatives journal, November 23–December 18, 1829, 99, 214, South Carolina Archives.

2. This is perhaps a reference to David Walker's *Appeal to the Colored Citizens of the World*, which was first published in Boston in September 1829, though the first copies of the book likely did not appear in the South until after this petition. See Peter P. Hinks, *To Awake My Afflicted Brethren: David Walker and the Problem of Antebellum Slave Resistance* (University Park: Pennsylvania State University Press, 1997), 118–19.

3. "An Act to Increase the Punishment Inflicted on Persons Convicted of Murdering Any Slave," which read:

> Be it enacted by the honorable the Senate and House of Representatives, now met and sitting in General Assembly, and by the authority of the same, That if any person, from and after the passing of this Act, shall willfully, maliciously, and deliberately murder any slaves within this State, such person, on conviction, shall suffer death without the benefit of clergy.

And be it further enacted by the authority aforesaid, That if any person shall kill any slave in sudden heat and passion, such person, on conviction, shall be fined in a sum not exceeding five hundred dollars and be imprisoned not exceeding six months.

In the Senate House, the twentieth day of December, in the year of our Lord one thousand eight hundred and twenty-one, and in the forty-sixth year of the Independence of the United States of America.

Benjamin Huger, President of the Senate

Patrick Noble, Speaker of the House of Representatives. (David J. McCord, *The Statutes at Large of South Carolina* [Columbia, S.C.: A. S. Johnston, 1839], 6:158)

There were at least some prosecutions of white people under this act, and their convictions were upheld by the South Carolina Appeals Court; see Helen Tunnicliff Catterall, *Judicial Cases Concerning American Slavery and the Negro* (Shannon: Irish University Press, 1968), 322–23, 356.

5.27] *A New York newspaper reports on maroons in Christ Church Parish*[1]

From the Charleston Mercury.

We learn from an attentive friend at Santee, that a large gang of runaway negroes, who have infested the Parishes of Christ Church and St James, (Santee) for several months, and committed serious depredations on the properties of the planters, was recently accidentally discovered by a party of gentlemen whilst out in the pursuit of deer. There were four or five camps, containing in all not less than twenty negroes. One of the fellows, in consequence of his own obstinacy and audacity, was fired at by one of the party, and killed. The rest retreated, and all succeeded in effecting their escape, except four, who are said to belong to a gentleman of this city. There are several other particulars given in the communication, which we deem it unnecessary to mention. We trust that the inhabitants of the Parishes will not cease their exertions until the evil shall be effectually removed.

1. *New York Evening Post*, August 10, 1829.

Afterword

Instances of marronage might seem episodic to historians, but our impression of maroon communities is shaped significantly by the limitations of source materials that deny us any sense of continuity over time. The sheer persistence of maroons who carved out their own space inside South Carolina will never truly be known since the individuals concerned left no written records, but the documents in this collection demonstrate that maroon communities existed in South Carolina from the early eighteenth century until at least 1830. Maroons also caused problems in several other states in the American South, particularly Florida, North Carolina, and Louisiana, but marronage was especially extensive and chronic in South Carolina. In part this was due to the geography of lowcountry South Carolina, which was particularly conducive to the formation of maroon communities. The flat coastal plain extended inland about fifty miles from the Atlantic, and according to one visitor, "About one-third of this plain consists of immense swamps, which, interlocking with each other, form part of a long chain, which stretches for several hundred miles along the coast of Georgia and the Carolinas."[1] While rice cultivation quickly tamed tidal river swamps, the plantations that were created on South Carolina's major rivers in the eighteenth and nineteenth centuries often fronted the rivers and backed onto yet more swamps.

These "back swamps" were different from the river swamps because despite both being areas of low, marshy ground, the stagnant water of back swamps rendered them unsuitable for rice cultivation. To planters, the back swamps, often dominated by large cypress trees, were of little productive use and were consequently ignored. This neglect left many spaces for maroons to occupy and make their own. Thus, while the plantations were places of order and regimentation, the back swamps remained marginal areas untamed by Europeans, densely forested, and full of dangerous fauna such as alligators and snakes. Since planters often owned large tracts of land, the typical layout of a plantation involved a "big house" close to the river and a "settlement" for the slaves, often some distance away. This arrangement often placed the enslaved close to the swamps and gave them the opportunity to become familiar with these

River swamp on the South Carolina side of the Savannah River. The high-tide mark can be seen on the trees. Photograph by the editor

marginal landscapes. As one historian has noted, these woods and swamps were liminal areas "that planters owned but that slaves had mastered."[2] It is all too easy for contemporary maps to give the impression that white mastery extended over the entire landscape, but the documents presented in this book suggest that white control over these areas was loose at best.

The documents in the preceding chapters suggest that before about 1830 marronage was comparatively common in South Carolina. There were many swamps where runaways could hide, and whites were seemingly powerless to stop them. After 1830 the records are almost, but not quite, silent on marronage. Periodic reports of maroon activity still cropped up: planters on the South Carolina side of the Savannah River in 1846, for example, complained of "serious crimes [committed] by desperate gangs of runaways, who are becoming more numerous, more reckless and are almost entirely secure from apprehension in our swamps," while maroons encamped in Coosawatchie Swamp in Beaufort District during the Civil War were reported to be "all armed with guns and pistols."[3] However, in general, the papers of the South Carolina legislature, newspapers, and private correspondence, which have been the main sources for information on marronage in this book, fall silent on the matter for the years after 1830. Are we to deduce from this that marronage came to an end or was at the very least significantly diminished after 1830? While absence from the historical record does not necessarily equate to the end of marronage, certainly maroons caused far fewer problems to white authorities after 1830 than they had before.

It is possible that maroons after 1830 became far more adept at hiding their locations from whites and isolated themselves more effectively from plantation society. In the summer of 1861 planters near Marion, close to the North Carolina border, "went in search of runaways who were thought to be in a swamp two miles from here.[4] A trail was discovered which, winding about much, conducted the party to a knoll in the swamp on which corn, squashes, and peas were growing and a camp had been burnt. Continuing the search, another patch of corn, etc., was found and a camp from which several negroes fled, leaving two small negro children, each about a year old.... There were several guns fired at the negroes who fled from the camp but none proved effectual. The camp seemed well provided with meal, cooking utensils, blankets, etc. The party returned, having taken the two children, twelve guns and one axe."[5] This report is reminiscent of those a generation earlier in the 1820s but is the only reference to a maroon camp of any size in South Carolina after 1830.

If, instead of better concealment, there were simply fewer maroons after 1830, then some tentative explanations suggest themselves. The demography of coastal South Carolina did not change radically between 1830 and 1860 except in one respect: the proportion of the population that was enslaved fell slightly overall, but this was mainly due to white immigration into Charleston. In rural areas roughly 80 percent of the population remained in bondage. Admittedly there were sixteen thousand more white people in the lowcountry in 1860 than in 1830, and demand for new farmsteads might have encroached on isolated areas popular with maroons. However, half of these sixteen thousand white immigrants lived in Charleston, so the impact of just eight thousand people spread over about five thousand square miles would not have been significant. Many areas popular with maroons—for example, the Savannah River islands near Purrysburg and the swamps on the north side of the Santee River—were never cultivated, and they remain pristine to this day.

There is also little sense that whites tightened their control over slave labor during the late antebellum period, either by enacting new laws or by mounting more patrols. Naturally whites were more vigilant during times of alarm, such as in the aftermath of the Nat Turner rebellion in Virginia in 1831, but this was never sustained for a lengthy period of time. The only significant change in the antebellum slave population was the inevitable decline in the proportion of

African-born slaves following the close of the Atlantic slave trade in 1808. The influx of 40,000 new Africans into South Carolina just prior to 1808 did momentarily halt this decline, and it would be easy to attribute the resurgence of marronage between 1813 and 1829 to these African-born slaves. However, none of the documents in chapter 5 mention the ethnicity of the maroons, so this must remain speculative, and the fact remains that in 1860 the vast majority of the 120,000 people enslaved in the lowcountry were African American, born into slavery. Elsewhere in the Americas creole slaves did not have quite the same propensity for marronage as the African-born since they often had familial bonds that flight would jeopardize, and they would also be surrendering the familiar for the unknown and running the risk of being killed by militia units or patrols. Some planters went out of their way to create economic incentives for the enslaved to remain on the plantations. One widely read agricultural journal advised, "no Negro, with a well stocked poultry house, a small crop advancing, a canoe partly finished, or a few tubs unsold, all of which he calculates soon to enjoy, will ever run away."[6] Conversely, however, creoles had the advantage of detailed local knowledge of the swamps where maroons found refuge, and so they could more easily take advantage of the hidden pathways through those areas.

Some fugitive slaves possibly found a better alternative to life in the swamps in the later antebellum era. The rise of militant abolitionism in the North after 1830 meant that runaway slaves from the South could find permanent sanctuary in Philadelphia or Boston, where lawyers would defend them from the perils of the Fugitive Slave Act. Published narratives by successful runaways such as Charles Ball (1837) and later Frederick Douglass (1845) showed that escape to the North was possible, and given the fact that information spread rapidly among enslaved populations, it is highly unlikely that owners managed to keep their slaves in the dark about successful fugitives. However, there is little evidence that this was actually happening. The five hundred miles that separated even the most northerly South Carolina slave from a free state meant that it was surely far more likely that fugitives remained fairly near the places from which they had fled. The smattering of evidence for the thirty years between 1830 and 1860 suggests that this was so.

Whether marronage actually declined after 1830 can never be completely determined. What is certain, given the material presented in this book, is that marronage was a far more serious problem for eighteenth- and early nineteenth-century South Carolina than has hitherto been acknowledged, involving more maroons in more locations and over a longer period of time than any history of slavery in the state has indicated. Every maroon community described in these documents preexisted the first mention of them, and it is impossible to know if maroons had only recently constructed settlements when they first appeared in the written records, perhaps a few weeks or months before, or had been resident in the swamps for many years. Maroons whose camps were far from white settlements and who refrained from raiding plantations for recruits or supplies, preferring instead to trade peaceably, if clandestinely, with slaves for items they needed, could conceivably have existed for long periods of time. Whites may or may not have known that maroons hid in the swamps, but even if they did know, it took a major logistical effort to organize militias for an expedition against them.

One of the major differences between whites' attempts to tackle marronage in the nineteenth century and those in the eighteenth century was that it was no longer possible to summon Indian tribes to hunt maroons in lowcountry swamps. Whites had used different Native American groups before 1787, freely acknowledging that they possessed "superior knowledge of the Woods and Swamps" and better tracking and survival skills than European settlers.[7] There is some evidence that eighteenth-century whites deliberately cultivated the "natural Dislike and Antipathy" that seemed to exist between their African slaves and Native American tribes. Certainly in neighboring North Carolina it was believed that far more slaves would flee into the woods and swamps "were they not so much afraid of the Indians, who have such a natural aversion to the Blacks, that they commonly shoot them when ever they find them in the Woods or solitary parts of the country." South Carolina resident George Milligen Johnston commented matter-of-factly that "it can never be in our Interest to extirpate them [Native Americans], or to force them from their lands; their Ground would soon be taken up by runaway Negroes from our settlements, whose Numbers would daily increase, and quickly become more formidable Enemies than Indians can ever be, as they speak our Language, and would never be at a Loss for Intelligence."[8] By the nineteenth century, however, there were no remaining Native Americans in the lowcountry, and even the Catawba, who had gained a particular reputation as effective maroon hunters and as "a brave and Warlike people and firmly attatched to the English," had been so reduced by disease that they were no longer able to help.[9] As a result whites were thrown back entirely to their own resources, and as the antebellum documents suggest, these resources were pretty slim. Judging from the limited success that militia units had in tracking down maroons when expeditions were ultimately deemed necessary, it is fairly evident that whites had little practical knowledge of the swamps. Moreover, hunting maroons was fraught with danger. Not only were maroons often armed and likely to fight back, but also rattlesnakes abounded to bite the unwary and alligators lay in wait for those wading across small creeks. In addition, it was all too easy to get lost.[10]

Given their own inadequacies, it is not surprising that white planters turned to enslaved people to help in the hunt for maroons. The willing and unwilling involvement of slaves in the recapture of maroons raises important questions about the relationship between the two groups. The demarcation between a plantation slave and a maroon is, of course, not as clear-cut as the label suggests. The former became the latter by running away and staying away; the latter could become the former by being captured. The two came from the same African and African American population in South Carolina and were familiar with each other's lives. It seems fairly clear that many plantation slaves sheltered and supported local maroons through trade in foodstuffs and other goods, by warning them when whites were closing in and, perhaps most important, by keeping their mouths shut. English visitor James Silk Buckingham was told by lowcountry slaveholders that "the negroes were often in the habit of stealing cattle from their masters' plantations . . . some being given to runaway negroes, who were often secretly sustained in this manner."[11] Maroons, on the other hand, were living embodiments of African American freedom who were able to offer plantation slaves the hope that one day they too could escape slavery. Africans still residing on the plantations and those hiding in the swamps often shared a common antipathy toward slavery and slave owners, and when a chance to strike back against those who had held them in bondage arose, the two had an obvious incentive for a common cause. However, several of the maroons in this book were captured or killed because of the intervention of blacks: Joe, for instance, who terrorized the Santee River planters in the 1820s, was killed only after he was lured out of hiding to trade with an enslaved boatman. Some slaves were no doubt forced to join in the hunt for maroons, but others chose to look out for themselves and joined whites voluntarily. Offers of money or freedom were no doubt attractive to some plantation slaves in return for their cooperation against maroons, but others were perhaps angered by the disruption to river traffic (especially if they worked on the rivers), by the repression that often followed raiding by maroons, or by maroons forcibly recruiting friends or family from plantations against their will. Maroons were not above attacking and killing slaves who got in their way. We should therefore be cautious about ascribing a group consciousness to all African Americans in South Carolina—clearly some enslaved people had just as much cause to abhor the actions of maroons as whites did.

Since hunting maroons was dangerous, both for whites and for slaves who assisted them, it is not surprising that when the threat posed or the damage caused by the maroons was not significant, some planters concluded that it was simply too much trouble to try to capture them. It was far easier to hope, however naively, that the fugitives would return home voluntarily. Judging from the petitions sent to the South Carolina legislature that have been included in this volume (documents 5.2–5.5, 5.9, and 5.22), planters were far from pleased when their slaves, which they considered their property, were killed by the militia, and some perhaps believed that the maroons should have been left alone. An additional reason for inertia was that days spent hunting maroons were days lost from managing the plantations, which might mean that remaining slaves were able to damage crops, and therefore profits, either through willful vandalism or, perhaps more likely, through simple inaction while unsupervised. It is doubtful, therefore, that many whites ventured anywhere near the swamps, except when they absolutely had to, and these zones in effect became spaces that were traversed and occupied only by Africans and African Americans. South Carolina's swamps had become locations that existed outside of the plantation society created by whites, functioning like tiny microstates independent of the larger polity. As places that offered refuge from unrelenting drudgery and torment, swamps competed successfully for the attention of the enslaved throughout the eighteenth and early nineteenth centuries, despite the dangers of their less than hospitable environment. Maroons were able to adapt to life in South Carolina's swamps, making the most of the opportunities offered and creating communities that offered self-determination and self-respect to the previously enslaved.

1. Adam Hodgson, *Letters from North America, Written during a Tour in the United States and Canada* (London: Hurst, Robinson, & Co., 1824), 104.

2. S. Max Edelson, *Plantation Enterprise in Colonial South Carolina* (Cambridge, Mass.: Harvard University Press, 2006), 67.

3. *Preamble and Regulations of the Savannah River Anti-Slave Traffick Association* (n.p., [1846]); Thomas G. Allen to General Walker, February 3, 1863, in Francis W. Pickens and Milledge L. Bonham Papers, Library of Congress, letter cited in Charles Joyner, "The World of the Plantation Slaves," in *Before Freedom Came: African-American Life in the Antebellum South*, ed. Edward C. Campbell and Kym S. Rice (Richmond, Va.: Museum of the Confederacy, 1991), 95–96.

4. Quite possibly this swamp was adjacent to the Pee Dee River, which formed the boundary between Marion and Horry counties.

5. *Marion Star*, June 18, 1861; printed in H. M. Henry, *The Police Control of the Slave in South Carolina* (1914; repr., New York: Negro Universities Press, 1968), 121. The original of this edition of the *Marion Star* has not been located at any archive in South Carolina. It is possible that Henry consulted a copy held in private hands.

6. *Southern Agriculturalist* 1 (1828): 525.

7. Milling, *Red Carolinians*, 227; James Glen to the duke of Newcastle, April 14, 1748, U.K. National Archives, CO 5/389, 58.

8. John Brickell, *The Natural History of North Carolina* (Dublin: James Carson, 1737), 263; George Milligen Johnston, *A Short Description of the Province of South Carolina* (London: John Hinton, 1770), 26. See also William S. Willis, "Divide and Rule: Red, White and Black in the Southeast," *Journal of Negro History* 48 (July 1963): 157–76; and James H. Merrell, "The Racial Education of the Catawba Indians," *Journal of Southern History* 50 (August 1984): 363–84.

9. James Glen to the duke of Newcastle.

10. For the remarkable story of Sarah Reimshart, who before being found was lost for more than two weeks in the woods in Effingham County, Georgia, close to where the Savannah River maroons were located, see *Gazette of the State of Georgia,* March 1, 1787.

11. James Silk Buckingham, *The Slave States of America* (London: Fisher, 1842), 1:86–87.

FURTHER READING

Aptheker, Herbert. "Additional Data on American Maroons." *Journal of Negro History* 32 (October 1947): 452–60.
———. *American Negro Slave Revolts.* New York: Columbia University Press, 1943.
———. "Maroons within the Present Limits of the United States." *Journal of Negro History* 24 (April 1939): 167–84.
Dusinberre, William. *Them Dark Days: Slavery in the American Rice Swamps.* New York: Oxford University Press, 1996.
Edelson, S. Max. *Plantation Enterprise in Colonial South Carolina.* Cambridge, Mass.: Harvard University Press, 2006.
Franklin, John Hope, and Loren Schweninger. *Runaway Slaves: Rebels on the Plantation.* Oxford: Oxford University Press, 1999.
Frey, Sylvia R. *Water from the Rock: Black Resistance in a Revolutionary Age.* Princeton, N.J.: Princeton University Press, 1991.
Hadden, Sally. *Slave Patrols.* Cambridge, Mass.: Harvard University Press, 2001.
Heuman, Gad, ed. *Out of the House of Bondage: Runaways, Resistance and Marronage in Africa and the New World.* London: Frank Cass, 1986.
Johnson, Michael P. "Runaway Slaves and the Slave Communities in South Carolina, 1799–1830." *William and Mary Quarterly* 38 (July 1981): 418–41.
Jones, Norrece T., Jr. *Born a Child of Freedom, Yet a Slave: Mechanisms of Control and Resistance in Antebellum South Carolina.* Hanover and London: Wesleyan University Press, 1990.
Joyner, Charles. *Down by the Riverside: A South Carolina Slave Community.* Urbana: University of Illinois Press, 1984.
Littlefield, Dan C. *Rice and Slaves: Ethnicity and the Slave Trade in Colonial South Carolina.* Baton Rouge: Louisiana State University Press, 1981.
Meaders, Daniel E. "South Carolina Fugitives as Viewed through Local Colonial Newspapers with Emphasis on Runaway Notices, 1732–1801." *Journal of Negro History* 60 (April 1975): 288–317.

Morgan, Philip D. "Colonial South Carolina Runaways: Their Significance for Slave Culture." *Slavery and Abolition* 6 (December 1985): 57–78.

———. *Slave Counterpoint: Black Culture in the Eighteenth Century Chesapeake and Lowcountry.* Chapel Hill: University of North Carolina Press, 1998.

Mulroy, Kevin. *Freedom on the Border: The Seminole Maroons in Florida, the Indian Territory, Coahuila and Texas.* Lubbock: Texas Tech University Press, 1993.

Olwell, Robert. *Masters, Slaves and Subjects: The Culture of the Power in the South Carolina Lowcountry, 1740–1790.* Ithaca, N.Y.: Cornell University Press, 1998.

Price, Richard. *The Guiana Maroons: A Historical and Bibliographical Introduction.* Baltimore & London: Johns Hopkins University Press, 1976.

———, ed. *Maroon Societies: Rebel Slave Communities in the Americas.* 2nd ed. Baltimore and London: Johns Hopkins University Press, 1979.

Schweninger, Loren. "Slave Independence and Enterprise in South Carolina, 1780–1865." *South Carolina Historical Magazine* 93 (April 1992): 101–25.

Smith, Mark M., ed. *Stono: Documenting and Interpreting a Southern Slave Revolt.* Columbia: University of South Carolina Press, 2005.

Wood, Peter. *Black Majority: Negroes in Colonial South Carolina from 1670 through the Stono Rebellion.* New York: Norton, 1974.

Index

Abercorn, Ga., 59, 64; swamp, 61
Abercorn Creek, Ga., 36, 59
Abercorn Island, Ga., 40
Alabama, xix
Andrew, 37
Ashepoo River, 21, 78, 86–88

Baldway, Obediah, 42
battles with maroons, 44–45, 57–60
Bear Creek, S.C., 58
Beaufort, S.C., 23, 33, 36, 68
Beaufort District, S.C., 3, 129
Beaufort Grand Jury, 36
Berisford, Richard, 9
Ben (1751), 14
Ben (1765), 20–21
Bennett, Gov. Thomas, 97–99, 104–5, 107, 115; proclamation, 98; report, 106–7
Berkley County Militia, 70–71
Billy, 110
Boston Evening Post, article, 30–1
Bourguin, John Lewis, letter 48–49
Bowen, Commodore Oliver, 57, 63, 67
Brailsford, Edward, petitions, 83–86
Brazil (quilombos), xiii–xv
Bristol (alias Brister), 81–82
British America, xv–xvi
Broughton, Gov. Thomas, 10–11
Brown, Joseph Chandler, 76–77
Brown, Mrs. Major, petition, 75–77
Buckingham, James Silk, 133
Bull, Lt. Gov. William, 16, 18, 25–26, 28–31; letter of, 23, 31

Bulloch (alias Bullock), Archibald, petition, 21
Butler, Capt. Elisha, 14–15
Butler, Ensign William, 14

Caesar, 36–38
Carnes, Capt. Henry, 96–97, declaration, 99
Catawba Indians, 23–33, 48, 53–54, 58, 69, 132
Charleston, S.C., 3–6, 10, 12, 16, 21, 23, 31, 39–42, 48, 50, 68, 70, 72–75, 78, 81, 83–85, 88, 98–99, 104–6, 109, 112, 114, 122–23, 127, 130
Chatham County (Ga.) Grand Jury, presentment, 44
Chicheum, 63–65
Christ Church Parish maroons, 39–42; petition concerning, 122–27
Claremont District, S.C., 107, 112, 115, 118
Clarendon District, S.C., 115, 118
Coachman, James, 11
Colleton County, S.C., maroons, 21–30, 78, 86–88
Colleton County regiment, 26
Colleton District Grand Jury, 79–80
Colly, 21
Columbian Blues, 101
Combahee River, 21, 86
compensation paid, 9; petitions for, 14–15, 21, 67, 75–77, 80–88, 91–93
Cork, 21
Culiatt, Adam, 75–76

140] INDEX

Culiatt, Ava, 75–76
Cupid, 63
Cuthbert, George, 20

Dasher, Capt. John Martin, 60
Dembo, 64
Dick, 64–65
Drayton, John, 37
Drayton, Gov. John, letter from, 74
Drayton, William, 70
Drayton Hall, 36–37
Dubose, Isaac, 91
Dubose, Samuel, 90–91, 118
Dubose, William, 110, 118
Dunmore, Gov., 39
Dunmore (maroon leader), 87–8
Dutch, Elizabeth, 9

Ebenezer, 13, 33, 40, 59, 61
Edisto River, 21, 25, 36
Elfe, Lt., 45
execution of maroons, 36–38, 66, 101, 113–15

First Maroon War (Jamaica), xv–xvi
Florida, xix–xx, 6, 12, 128
Ford, George, 93–104, 106–8, 110, 112, 115–6, 118, 120
Fortune, 63
Frank, 64
French America, xii–xiii
Fron, king of the Catawba, 28–29

Gabriel, 81–82
Gaillard, James, 90, 117
Gaillard, Thomas, 91, 110–11, 118
"General of the Swamps," xviii
Georgetown, S.C., 3, 90–91, 95–98, 100–108, 115, 119–20; maroons near, 95–98, 120–22
Georgia, vii, xix–xx, 13, 16–18, 33, 35, 37, 39–40, 43–49, 56, 58, 62–63, 66–67, 69, 72, 88, 128; maroons in, 17–21, 33–36, 40–70, 122, 129–30
Georgia House of Assembly, resolution of, 17–18

Georgia Council, discussions of, 34–35, 66
Georgia Grand Jury, presentment, 35–36, 39
Glen, Gov. James, 12
grand jury presentments, 35–36, 39, 79–80
Granville County (S.C.) Militia, 21, 45, 47–49, 53–58, 64, 68–70
Guerard, Godin, 61, 64, 67
Guerard, Jacob, 46
Gunn, Col. James, 58–61

Haiti, xiii, xvi, 72. See also St. Domingue
Hartstone, Joachim, 45, 48–49; letter, 49
Hector, 14
Herriat, 64
Hirschman (alias Hersman), John Casper, 63–65
Howell, Lt. Col., 58–59
Huggins, Col., 106, 120
Hughes, Arthur, 73–74
Hutson, Col. Thomas, 52–53, 56–58, 68

insurrection rumors, 5–6, 23–28, 30–32, 47, 53, 68, 72, 74–75, 79
Isaac, 38
Isham, 111–12

Jack, aided capture of maroons, 119–20
Jack: execution, 95–99, 101; reprieve, 95–96, 103–4
Jackson, Col. George, 25–27
Jackson, Gen. James, 44–47, 58; letters from, 45–47
Jamaica, x, xiii, xv–xvi, 4, 60, 62, 100, 104
Jemmy, 63
Joe, 63–64
Joe (alias Forest), 93–120, 133
John, 19
Johnson, George Milligen, 132
Juliet, 61, 63–65

Kelvert, William, petition 14–15

Laurens, Henry, letter from, 31
legislative action against maroons, 8–12, 17–21, 24–30, 49–51, 68–71

Lemden, Lt., 58
Little Cook, 64
Louisiana, xix
Lowerman (alias Lourman), John, 63–65, 67
Louis (alias Lewis), 57, 60–67; trial record of, 62–65

Massachusetts Centinel, article, 67
Manchester, S.C., 107–8, 112
Marion maroons, 130
Matthews, Governor George, 47, letter from, 58
maroons: armed, xi, xviii, xxi, 11, 18, 37, 45–46, 49–52, 55–56, 68–79, 74, 78–80, 90–92, 96, 102–7, 122, 129, 132; boats owned by, 18–20, 35–36, 45, 60, 64, 80, 121; camps of, xvi, xviii, 3, 6–7, 11–12, 14, 19–20, 35–38, 42, 44–47, 57–61, 63–66, 70, 79, 93, 98, 106–7, 110, 112–17, 120–22, 127, 129–30, 132; crops grown by, xvii, xix, 20, 45, 59, 63–64, 101, 121, 130; decline of, 128–34; definition of, ix; depredations, xviii, 17–20, 35, 37, 39, 46–56, 80, 85, 87, 91, 96, 98, 105–6, 108, 100, 120, 123–25, 127; possessions of, 20, 37, 45–47, 59–60, 105, 122; relations with Native Americans, 132; relations with slaves, 132–33
marronage: in Alabama, xix; in Brazil (*quilombos*), xiii–xv; British America, xv–xvi, in Florida, xix–xx; in French America, xii–xiii; in Louisiana, xix; in North Carolina, xvii–xix, 132; in Spanish America (*palenques*), x–xi; in Surinam, xii, 60; in Virginia, xvi–xvii
McGillivray, Lachlan, 20
McIntosh, Roderic, letter from, 18–19
McLeod, John, petition, 14–15
McPherson, Maj., 58–59
Middleton, Col. Thomas, 21
militia action against maroons, 10–11, 21, 35–36, 44–47; 57–60, 132
Montaigut, David, 63, 66
Mose, Fort (Florida), xix–xx
Mosquito Indians, xv

Native Americans: as allies of maroons, xiv–xv, xx; hunting maroons, xv, 11–12, 23–33, 48, 53–54, 58, 69, 132. *See also* Catawba Indians; Mosquito Indians; Notchee Indians; Seminole Indians
newspaper reports of maroon activity, 42, 44–45, 57, 59–61, 67, 75–76, 95–97, 100–105, 107–8, 112–13, 120–22
Newton, 121
New York Evening Post, article, 127
North Carolina, xvii–xix, 32, 72, 102, 128, 130, 132
Notchee Indians, 11–12, 23
Nunes, Moses, 35

O'Driscoll, Matthew, petition, 80–83
Old Hal, xix

Pee Dee River, 121
Peggy, 61, 64
Perrin, Mrs., 117–19
Perry, Sarah, 9
Philadelphia Gazette, article, 75
Pinckney, Gov. Thomas, 45–46, 50, 53–56, 68, 70; letters, 53–54, 56; proclamation 55
Pineville, S.C., 89–90, 109–13
Pineville Police Association, 109–11
Pompey, 92–93
Pope, 64
Porcher, Peter, 50
Porcher, Samuel, 90, 111–12, 118
Porcher, Thomas, 90, 109, 118; journal entry, 111–12
Purrysburgh, S.C., 40, 46, 53, 55, 57, 59, 68, 130

Raoul, Dr. Lewis, 108; petition of, 113–15
Ravenel, Daniel, 85
Ravenel, Henry, 90, 117; diary entry, 90–91
Ravenel, John, 90, 113, 117
Reed, Josiah, 38
rewards: given, 9, 13, 28, 33, 99, 119; offered, 10, 18, 25–26, 35, 38, 44, 47–48, 51–55, 73–74, 93, 98, 103, 107–8, 110, 115, 119; sought, 119

rice cultivation, xvi, xviii, 3–4, 20, 32, 45–46, 48, 59, 64, 121, 128
Richardson, Col. J. B., 108, 112
Richland District, S.C., 115–19
Rodgers, David, petition of, 91–93
royal petitions to free, 114–19
Russell, Capt. Charles, 10

St. Andrew's Parish, 105–6
St. Augustine, Fla., xix–xx, 12
St. Bartholomew's Parish, S.C., 26, 39, 78, 81
St. Domingue (Haiti), xiii
St. George's Parish, S.C. 84
St. James Santee Parish, S.C., 83, 85, 99–100, 103, 118, 127
St. John's Parish, S.C., 42, 76, 115
St. Paul's Parish, S.C., 36
St. Stephen's Parish, S.C., 91, 114, 115, 118
St. Thomas's Parish, S.C., 104
Sam, 38
Sancho, 38
Santee Canal, 41, 98, 110–13
Santee River maroons, 88–120, 130
Savannah, Ga., 16–18, 33; siege of, 39–40
Savannah light infantry, 45, 58–60
Savannah River maroons, 17–21, 33–36, 40–70, 122, 129–30
Sebastian, the "Spanish Negro," 8–9
Seminole Indians, xx
Scheuber, Justus, H., 63, 66
Sharper (alias Capt. Cudjoe), 60–65
slavery in South Carolina: origins, 1; development, 1–3; laws regulating, 5, 9–10; number of Africans enslaved, 3; 130–31; proportion of the population enslaved, 3; punishment regimes 4–5, 36; resistance to, 5–6, 12–13, 124; runaways, ix, 6–7, 40, 73–74; in urban areas, 4
South Carolina Assembly: action against maroons, 8–11, 24–30, 49–51, 69–70; petitions to, 80–88, 91–93, 115–19, 122–26
South Carolina Council: debates action against maroons 51–52, 70–71; report on the North Carolina boundary, 32–33; resolution, 11–12

South Carolina Senate, debates cost of fighting maroons, 68–69
Spanish America, x–xi
Stephens, Col. Jacob, 29
Stephens, William, 63, 66
Stephon, 113–15
Stono rebellion, 5, 12–13
Stono swamp maroons, 14–15, 36–37, 70, 105
Surinam, xii, 60

Tattnall, Capt., 58–59
Telfair, Gov. Edward, proclamation, 47–48
Theron, 20
Three-Fingered Jack, 100, 104
Tilly, 38
tobacco cultivation, xvi
Tom, 119–20
trials of maroons, 60–65, 97
Tuffe, 38

Ulmer, Philip, 61, 63–65

Vanderhorst, Col. Arnoldus, 70, 74, 125
Virginia, xvi–xvii

Washington Greens, 96, 101, 104
Will, 121
Williams, Gov. David, message of, 86–87
Williams, Joseph, 41–42
Williams, Meshack, 93; claim of, 99–100
Williamsburg District, S.C., 90–93, 103
Williamson, Champion, 20
Winkler, Capt. Jacob, 57, 64, 69
Wolmar (alias Walthour) John, 45–47, 63
Wright, Gov. James, 16, 21, 39; letter from, 18–19
Wright, Capt. Richard, 11
Wyley, Alexander, deposition taken by, 20–21
Wyley, Samuel, 24–25, 27–29

Young, Isaac, 19

Zubley's Ferry, 58

ABOUT THE EDITOR

TIMOTHY JAMES LOCKLEY is an associate professor of history at the University of Warwick, England, and a specialist in the history of the American South. He is the author of *Welfare and Charity in the Antebellum South* and *Lines in the Sand: Race and Class in Lowcountry Georgia, 1750–1860* and coeditor with Catherine Armstrong and Roger Fagge of *America in the British Imagination*.

www.ingramcontent.com/pod-product-compliance
Lightning Source LLC
Chambersburg PA
CBHW021735220426
43662CB00008B/867